汉英双语版

经验与教育
Experience and Education

【美】约翰·杜威　著

盛群力　译

中国轻工业出版社

图书在版编目（CIP）数据

经验与教育：汉英双语版/（美）约翰·杜威（John Dewey）著；盛群力译. —北京：中国轻工业出版社，2016.12（2022.8重印）

ISBN 978-7-5184-1134-4

Ⅰ.①经… Ⅱ.①约…②盛… Ⅲ.①英语－汉语－对照读物②杜威（Dewey, John 1859—1952）－实用主义教育思想 Ⅳ.①H319.4: G

中国版本图书馆CIP数据核字（2016）第237375号

总策划：石　铁
策划编辑：吴　红　　　　　　　责任终审：张乃柬
责任编辑：吴　红　　　　　　　责任监印：刘志颖

出版发行：中国轻工业出版社（北京东长安街6号，邮编：100740）
印　　刷：三河市鑫金马印装有限公司
经　　销：各地新华书店
版　　次：2022年8月第1版第3次印刷
开　　本：710×1000　1/16　印张：12.50
字　　数：107千字
书　　号：ISBN 978-7-5184-1134-4　定价：38.00元
读者热线：010-65125990，65262933　传真：010-65181109
发行电话：010-85119832　传真：010-85113293
网　　址：http://www.chlip.com.cn　http://www.wqedu.com
电子信箱：1012305542@qq.com
如发现图书残缺请与我社联系调换
160991Y1X101ZYW

"约翰·杜威是一位为自己所处时代的需求创造哲学思想的大家。就这种影响力而言,他可与先贤圣人奥古斯丁、阿奎纳、弗朗西斯·培根、笛卡尔、洛克和奥古斯特·孔德齐名。"

——阿尔弗雷德·诺斯·怀特海
(Alfred North Whitehead)

"约翰·杜威在美国教育理论和实践方面创造的深远影响力是毋庸置疑的。"

——威廉·赫德·基尔帕特里克
(William Heard Kilpatrick)

"约翰·杜威无疑是美国哲学史上的卓越人物,他是一个对自由文明的基本理念最充满活力的人。如果要授予他'国家哲学家'的称号,想必他也是当之无愧的。"

——莫里斯·R. 科恩
(Morris R. Cohen)

目　录

经验与教育（中文版）／1

序言 ··· 3
第一章　传统教育与进步教育 ································· 5
第二章　需要一种有关经验的理论 ························· 11
第三章　经验的标准 ··· 19
第四章　社会的控制 ··· 37
第五章　自由的性质 ··· 47
第六章　目的的意义 ··· 51
第七章　进步主义的教材组织 ······························· 57
第八章　经验——教育的方法和目标 ······················ 73

杜威生平与主要著作年表 ······································ 77

译后记 ·· 85

经验与教育（英文版）／89

Preface ·· 91
Chapter 1　Traditional vs. Progressive Education ········· 95

Chapter 2	The Need of a Theory of Experience	105
Chapter 3	Criteria of Experience	115
Chapter 4	Social Control	139
Chapter 5	The Nature of Freedom	153
Chapter 6	The Meaning of Purpose	159
Chapter 7	Progressive Organization of Subject-Matter	167
Chapter 8	Experience—The Means and Goal of Education	189

经验与教育

（中文版）

Experience and Education

【美】约翰·杜威 著

盛群力 译

序　言

　　一切社会运动都包含着各种冲突，这些冲突在思想上则表现为各种论战。教育是一项重要的社会福利事业，如果在教育领域内不存在理论的和实践的各种争斗，反而不太正常。各种实际的冲突及其所引起的各种论争，对理论而言，至少对构成教育哲学的理论而言，只是提出了一种问题。一种高明的教育理论的任务就在于探讨各种现实冲突的起因，然后比较代表各个论争派别的实践和思想，不偏向任何一方，提出一种更深刻的、更全面的实施计划。

　　教育哲学的任务并不是把对立的各派思想调和起来，寻求中庸之道，也不是将各派观点东拼西凑而加以折中合并。教育哲学的任务是需要引导出一套新的概念规则，以指导新型的实践模式。正因为如此，背离传统和习俗而建立一种教育哲学，是一件相当困难的事情。同样的道理，根据一套新的概念规则来管理学校，比因循守旧更为不易。所以，以一套新的思想和由新思想所引起的新活动为指导的各种运动，或迟或早都会回到过往的实践传统中去——当代教育又在企图恢复古希腊和中世纪的各种原理,这便是很好的例证。

因此,在本书的末尾,我提出建议,追寻新教育运动前景并且适应了新社会秩序的现实需要的人,应当只思考教育本身的含义,而无须顾及教育的各种"主义",甚至对"进步主义"也不必有所忌讳。因为,抛开教育本身的含义,任何以一种"主义"为思想和行动依据的运动,都会陷入对受到其他"主义"无形控制的运动的反击之中。这样一来,它的各项原理的形成只是基于反击对立面的非难,而不是出于对各种实际需要、问题和可能性加以综合的建设性调研。本书力图引起对教育问题更广泛的、更深入的关注,以提出适当的处置办法。果能如此,这便是本书的价值所在了。

约翰·杜威

第一章 传统教育与进步教育

人们总喜欢用两极对立的方式去思考问题。这样就形成了"非此即彼"的信念,认为在"此"与"彼"的两极中间没有其他的可能性。当被迫认识到这两极都行不通时,这个信念仍然让他们坚持认为自己在理论上是正确的,只是实际情况和环境迫使他们妥协。教育哲学也是如此。我们把教育理论的发展史标记为两种截然不同的观念,即教育的内发论和外铄论。也就是说:一种观点主张教育是基于人自身的天然禀赋;另一种观点认为教育是克服自然心向,在外部压力下获得习惯的过程。

目前,就学校的实际情况来说,这种对立倾向表现为传统教育和进步教育两者之间的分庭抗礼。如果对传统教育的基本理念不做精确阐述,那么可以概略表述如下:第一,教育材料是由以前所产生的知识和技能体系构成的,因此,学校的主要任务是把这些知识和技能传授给下一代。第二,在以前,学校也已经建立了行为准则和规范,要形成与这些行为规范和准则相一致的习惯,其内容之一就是道德训练。第三，学校组织（我所指的是学生之间和师生之间的关系）的一般模式构成了学校这类机构，这与其他社会机构极为不同。只要想象一下平时用的教室、课程时间表、班级划分、考试和升级的制度以及各种秩序规则，你就会理解"组织模式"的含义了。如果你把学校里的情景与家庭里的情景做一下比较，你就会理解学校明显不同于其他社会机构形式的含义了。

以上提及的三个特征就限定了学校教学和训练的目标及方法。其主要的目的或目标是使青年一代获得教材中有组织的知识体系和完备的技能，以便为承担未来的责任和取得生活上的成功做好准备。由于学科教材和规范行为的标准是从过去传承下来的，所以总的来说，学生必须具备温顺的、接受的、服从的态度。书籍，尤其是教科书，代表着前人的学问与智慧，而教师的作用在于把学生与教学材料有效地结合起来。通过教师，知识和技能得以传递，学生的行为规范得以强化。

我对当前的教育状况做了这样一个简要的概述，不是为了批判其背后的哲学。新教育和进步学校日益兴盛，正是对传统教育不满的结果，这本身就是对传统教育的一种批评。如果把这些隐约的批评明确地表示出来，可能就是这样的：从本质上来说，传统的教育体制是当权者和学校外部强加的产物。它把原本适用于成人的标准、教材和方法强加到那些正慢慢长大的孩子身上。成人和孩子之间的差别如此之大，因此那些教材、学习方法和行为规范对于孩子已有的能力来说都是很陌生的，其所要求的远远超出了学习者已经掌握的经验。因此，教师只能通过灌输的方式来进行教学，即使是优秀的教师也会使用艺术的手段来掩盖这种灌输，以此减轻它本身明显的残酷性。

但是，成熟的人或成年人制作的东西与年轻人的经验及能力之间隔着一道鸿沟，因此在这样的情况下，要想学生主动参与到教育的发展进程中，那是不可能的。学生的任务是学习，就如同士兵的任务是打仗直至战死一样。这里的学习意味着获得书本上和年长者头脑中的知识。并且，教师所教的内容基本上都是固定不变的。教学内容以成品的形式出现，人们既不去考虑它原来是怎么建构的，当然也不会去修改，即使将来这些内容确定是会变的。社会的文化产品尽量假设未来将跟过去非常相似，在一个变革是常态的社会里，仍旧以此作为教育材料。

如果谁试图把隐含在新教育实践里的教育哲学明确地表达出来，那么我认为，现在已经能在各种进步学校中发现某些共同的原则。主张学习者个性的表达与培养，反对根据当权者强加的意愿来培养；主张自由活动，反对受学校外部纪律的制约；主张通过经验学习，反对从教材和教师那里学习；主张从切身的重大需求出发来获得技能和技巧，而不是通过机械训练获得孤立的技能和技巧；主张利用好当前生活中存在的大部分机会，反对为或多或少有些遥远的未来做准备；主张所学的是一个不断变化的世界，反对固定不变的教学目的和内容。

以上列出的几条原则本身还是抽象的，它们只有在具体应用结果中才会变得具体。正因为所提出的这些原则是如此的基本和广泛，所以当把它们投入到学校和家庭实践中时，所有事情都依赖于如何对其做出合理的解释。正是在这一点上，之前提及的"非此即彼"的哲学才变得特别有市场。新教育的一般哲学可能是合理的，但是新教育的抽象原则之间的差别不能决定包含道德和理智取向的方式应该在实践中起作用。通常在一场新的运动中总会有危险存在，即原有的目的和方法会排斥新的目的和方法，新的运动在发展其原则时可能就会比较消极，缺乏积极和建设的性质。因此，在实践中，新的运动是从被抛弃的东西里获取解决问题的启示，而没有通过建设性地发展自己的哲学来加以完善。

我认为应该在这样的观念中发现新哲学的基本一致性：实际经验的过程和教育的过程之间有着密切且必然的联系。如果这一点是正确的，那么在积极并建设性地发展自己的基本观点时就要取决于对经验是否有一个正确的理念。例如，有关教材的组织问题（将会在后面章节中详细讨论）。进步教育的问题是：教材及其在经验中的组织这二者的意义和地位是什么？教材是如何起作用的？趋向于将其内容循序渐进地进行组织的经验中有没有内在固有的东西？当没有把经验的材料循序渐进地组织起来时会有什么后果？一种在排斥和完全对立的基础上发展起来的哲学将会忽视这些问题。该哲学将趋向于这样的假设：因为旧有的教育基于已有的组织，所以它会成功地排斥全部的组织原则，而不用努力去发现它在经验的基础上的含义以及获得的途径。我们也许能了解到新教育和旧教育之间所有的不同点并达成相似的结论。当摆脱了外部的控制时，问题就变成了在经验内部本身存在的控制中发现一些因素。当论及摆脱外部权威时，它并不是指要排斥所有的权威，而是需要搜寻一种更有效的权威的来源。不能因为旧有的教育把适用于成人的知识、方法和行为规则强加于儿童身上，就确定成人的知识和技能对于未成年人的经验来说没有指导价值，除非基于极端的"非此即彼"哲学。相反，相对于现有的传统学校来说，基于个人经验的教育可能就意味着成年人和儿童之间更多样化和更亲密的接触，结果儿童会得到别人更多而不是更少的指导。这样问题就变成了：成人和儿童之间应该怎样进行这样的接触，并且不违背通过个人经验学习的原则。这个问题的解决办法需要一种经过慎重考虑的能在个人经验的组成中起作用的有关社会因素的哲学。

前面所做的评论表明了新教育本身的基本原则不能解决有关进步学校的任何实践指导和管理问题。它们反而产生了一些新问题，需要依据一种新的经验哲学才能得到解决。如果认为只要抛弃旧教育的理念和实践然后走向与之对立的另一端就行，那么我们就还没有认识到这些问题，更谈不上什么解决了。然而，当我这样说——许多新式学校更愿意选择稍微经过组织或毫无组织的内容进行学习；许多新式学校更愿意这么做，好像成年人给予的任何形式的指引和指导都是对个体自由的侵犯，好像教育应该关注现在和未来这个观点意味着了解过去对教育几乎没有什么作用——的时候，我确定你就会理解它的含义了。我们不是要夸大缺点，只是想说明，一种教育理论和实践，如果只是消极地向前发展，或者只是针对教育中的现有状况做出相反的反应，而不是在经验理论及其教育潜能的基础上积极地、建设性地发展其目标、方法和教学内容，那么它将会意味着什么。

一种声称基于自由理念的教育哲学也可能变得教条，就如同我们曾反对过的传统教育那样，这么说一点也不过分。因为任何理论和实践，如果不对它们本身隐含的原则进行批判性检查，那么它们就是教条的。我们说新教育强调学习者的自由学习。这是对的。现在问题就来了：这里的自由是什么意思，并且要在什么情况下才能实现这样的自由？我们说在传统教育中普遍存在的这种外部的灌输，限制了而不是促进了儿童智力和道德的发展。这也是对的。认识到这个缺点后也会出现一个问题，即：教师和书本在促进儿童教育发展方面起了什么作用？承认传统教育运用了过多有关过去的事实和观点作为学习内容，几乎不会对处理现在与未来的问题有任何帮助。这是对的。现在我们就有了另外一个问题，即如何发现过去的成就与现在的问题之间实际存在于经验内部的联系。我们的问题是探究了解过去可能会如何转化成有效地处理未来问题的一种潜在的工具。我们也许反对把过去的知识作为教育的终点，然后以此仅仅强调将其作为工具的重要性。当我们这样做的时候，教育史上新的问题就出现了：年轻人应该以一种什么样的方式掌握过去的知识，而通过这种方式掌握过去就成了理解当前生活的一种有效的中介？

第二章 需要一种有关经验的理论

简而言之,我要说明的一点是,对那些坚信新教育的人来说,抛弃传统教育的哲学和实践会引起一些新的教育难题。如果我们未认清这个事实,未能彻底认识到摆脱过去并不能解决任何问题,那么,我们就是在盲目和混乱中行事。因此,在接下来的篇章中,我们将说明新教育中将会遇到的主要问题,并建议应该按照什么主线去寻找这些问题的解决方式。我认为在所有的不确定中会存在一个永恒性的参考框架,即:教育和个人经验之间的有机联系;或者,我假设新的教育哲学致力于一种经验的和实验的哲学。但是经验和实验不是一种自己能解释清楚的观点,其含义仍是将要探究的问题的一部分。为了明白经验主义的含义,我们需要理解什么是经验。

相信真正的教育来源于经验并不意味着所有的经验都是真正的或者都具有同样的教育意义。经验和教育不能直接互相等同起来。因为有些经验是没有教育意义的。任何一种没有教育意义的经验都会阻止或者干扰未来经验的积累。一种经验可能会这样变得麻木不仁：它可能会导致人缺乏灵敏度和同情心。这样以后要想再获得更丰富的经验就不可能了。除此之外，一种既定的经验可能增强了人在某一特殊方面的自动化技能，这样就会使他局限于惯例之中；这种影响同样能缩小以后经验的领域。有一种经验可能当时会让人觉得很愉快，但是它会促使人们形成松懈和粗心的态度；这种态度会改变随后的经验水平，以阻止人们获得经验应该给予他们的东西。此外，经验与经验之间也可能没有一点联系，因此即使任何一方都使人愉快甚至让人激动，它们也仍然不能相互连接并不断积累。这样人就浪费了精力，并变得思想分散。每一种经验都可能是生动的、鲜活的，并且会是"有趣的"，然而它们的分离状态可能会人为地产生分散的、碎片化的、脱离中心的习惯。养成这些习惯的结果是人们没有能力控制未来的经验。最终，它们会以一种让人高兴的方式或是让人不满并厌弃的方式离开，如同它们来的时候一样。在这样的情况下，再谈自我控制就没用了。

传统教育提供了大量的上面提及的各种经验的例子。传统的教室不是学生获得经验的地方，这一点甚至是被大家公认的，而这样的假设却是一个巨大的错误。然而，进步教育作为一个通过经验学习的计划，与旧教育是截然相反的。在传统教育里，学生和教师所具有的经验大部分是错误的，做出这种评断是恰当的。例如，有多少学生对观点毫无反应，有多少学生因为体验学习的方式而失去了学习的动力？有多少学生通过机械的训练获得了一些专门的技能，以致他们的判断力和在新情况下理智地行动的能力反而受到了限

第二章 需要一种有关经验的理论

制？有多少学生认为学习过程很无聊？有多少学生发现他们所学的内容与学校外面的生活情境是如此的不一致以至他们没有能力去控制后者？有多少学生慢慢地把读书当作一种乏味的苦差事，因此他们能受其他一切的"控制"，唯独不能接受华而不实的阅读材料？

我提出这些问题，不是要对旧教育做完全的否定，而是因为其他的目的。第一，我要强调的事实是年轻人在传统学校里确实是有经验的；第二，问题不是经验的缺乏，而是这些经验是不完整的并且是错误的——从与未来经验相连的角度来说是不完整的、错误的。这个观点积极的一面甚至比与进步教育的联系更重要。坚持经验的必要性是不够的，甚至在体验每一件事情时依赖经验品质的活动也是不够的。任何经验都有两个方面的特性。直接的一个方面是，这种经验是让人愉快的或讨厌的，而它对后续经验还会产生影响。这个方面很明显也很容易判断出来。一种经验的效果并不体现在它的表面。这就给教育者提出了一个问题。他们要安排一种经验，不排斥学生而是使其参与到活动中，比直接获得经验给学生带来的愉快感更多，因为它们促使学生以后能拥有令人满意的经验。没有人只为自己活着或死亡，同样，也没有经验单独存在或消失。每一种经验都是一种完全独立的要求或意愿，它们依赖未来经验而存在。因此，一种基于经验教育的中心问题是选择一些当前的经验，这些经验有创造性地对后来的经验起作用。

稍后，我应该更详细地讨论经验连续性的原则，或者可以称之为经验的连续统。这里我希望能简单地强调教育经验哲学中原则的重要性。如同其他任何理论一样，教育哲学也必须以文字和符号的形式表述出来。但是到目前为止，它已经不只是停留于口头形式，还是指导教育的一种计划。像任何计划一样，它必须形成一个用于参考的框架，明确什么应该做和怎么做。越是明确真诚地认为教育是在经验中、通过经验和为了经验而发展的，对经验的含义有一个清晰的概念也就越重要。除非把经验设想成一种计划的结果，并且这种计划是为了决定教学内容、教学和训练的方法、学校的材料设备和社会组织，要不然它便是空想。这种经验只是流于一种文字形式，可能有时候会让人情绪激动，但是也可能会被其他形式的文字取代，而且不同的文字形式区别不大，除非有具体的操作可以发起并运行。不能仅仅因为传统教育墨守着之前计划与程序的常规，就认为进步教育是毫无计划的即兴勾画。

一直以来，传统教育的发展都没有成熟的教育哲学的支持。它所需的是一系列抽象的话语，如文化、训练，我们伟大的文化遗产，等等，但是真正能指导传统教育的并不是它们，而是惯例和已经制定的常规。正因为进步学校不能依赖已经建立的传统和制度习惯，所以它们的运行，要么多多少少是有偶然因素的，要么是由理念指导的，当把这些理念明确连贯地表达出来时，就形成了一种教育哲学。对具有传统学校特征的组织表示不满，也就生发了对另一种基于理念的组织的需求。我认为，只要对教育历史稍稍有点熟悉，就能证明教育改革家和创新者也会觉得教育哲学是必需的。而那些坚

第二章 需要一种有关经验的理论

持已有系统的人只需要一些动人的话语来证明当前的实践。真正的工作都是根据习惯完成的，这些习惯如此地墨守成规最后就变成习以为常的了。进步教育告诉我们，教育哲学急切需要基于经验的哲学，而且这个急切程度比依靠以往的教育创新者更甚。

这里我要顺便提及，用林肯有关民主的释义来看以上所讨论的哲学，那么教育哲学是属于经验，或是由于经验而产生，抑或是为了经验的。不管是"属于""由于"还是"为了"，这些词没有一个通过名称就能自己表达清楚的。每一个词都是一种发现并把序列和组织原则投入实践的挑战，而这些序列和组织原则来源于对教育经验的理解。

相应的，要找出适合新教育的教材、教法及社会关系是比适应传统教育难得多的任务。我认为在管理进步学校过程中经历的许多困难以及反对他们的一些批评都源于这个原因。当人们认为新教育在某种程度上比旧教育更简单的时候，这些困难会加重而批评声也会增加。我想象一下，这个观点或多或少还是普遍存在的。也许它也再一次阐明了"非此即彼"的哲学，即来自这样的观点：在传统学校里所做的，在进步学校里就不能实施。

新教育原则上比旧教育要简单得多，这一点我欣然认同。新教育符合生长的原则，而旧教育在教材和教法的安排上很多都是人为仿造的，且人工的东西经常会导致简单的事情复杂化。但是容易和简单是不等同的。发现什么是真正简单的事情并根据这个发现去行动是一个非常困难的任务。一旦这些人工的和复杂的东西得以制度化并以惯例和常规固定下来，人们按照制度、惯例和常规去做，就要比采用新观点并从中发现实际问题简单得多。之前托勒密天文学体系中有关循环和回转圆的问题要比哥白尼学说中的问题更为复杂。但是实际的天文学现象组织在受到哥白尼学说影响之前，遵循旧有的智慧习惯路线做事，遇到的阻力最小，因而也是最简单的一条路线。因此，我们又回到这样的观点，即如果试图从一个新的方向去展开学校工作，那就需要一种连贯的经验理论，这种理论为选择与组织恰当的教学方法和教学材料提供了一个积极的方向。这个过程会很慢也很艰苦。这就是生长，而且在生长的过程中会有很多可能阻碍生长并使它偏离正确路线的障碍物。

我后面将会对组织做简单的阐述。也许，这里需要说的就是我们必须从这样的趋势中摆脱出来，即根据组织的种类来思考组织，也就是要避免代表着传统教育的内容（或者教学材料）、方法和社会关系的组织。我认为现在之所以存在许多有关反对组织的观点，是因为要想脱离旧学校学习的情境是很难做到的。一提起"组织"，我们就会自动地想到那种熟悉的组织，接着就会产生反感并对任何一种有关组织的观念都表示出畏缩心理。此外，势力不断增强的教育反对者把新型学校中缺乏合适的理智和道德组织作为证据，不仅想证明组织的必要性，而且把任何一种组织与实验科学兴起之前的组织等同起来。基于经验和实验建立有关组织的概念这一过程的失败，导致了那些反对者轻而易举地获得了胜利。但事实上，现在经验科学为我们提供了最好的理智组织，并且这种组织在任何领域中都可以找到，这些足以证明我们没有任何理由来说明我们为什么应该成为有关秩序和组织问题的"败将"。

第三章　经验的标准

前面已经讲到需要建立一种经验的理论以便教育能在此基础上合理地运行，倘若这种说法是真的，那么显然接下来要讨论的就是呈现建立这种理论所需要的一些最重要的原则。因此，我将不会因做了诸多哲学分析而表示歉意，因为如果不进行这些分析可能是行不通的。然而，我可以从某种程度上向您保证，做这种分析本身并不是目的，而是为了获得标准，对大多数人来说，这些标准以后会被用到许多具体的也很有趣的问题的讨论之中。

前面我已经提到过连续的范畴或者经验的连续性。正如我所指出的那样，当我们在教育过程中试图区分有价值的经验和无价值的经验时，往往会涉及这个原则。无须争辩，这种区分不仅对批判传统类型的教育是必需的，而且对创办和指导一种不同类型的教育也是必要的。然而，多多少少对这种想法的必要性进行一些研究也是可取的。我认为，可以安全地假设：一方面，进步教育运动较之于传统学校的实施过程似乎更符合人们所崇尚的民主主义思想，因为后者有如此多的独断和专制的性质。另一方面，进步教育运动之所以受到追捧，是因为其所用的方法很人性化，与之相比，传统学校的做法总是粗暴苛刻的。

我所关心的问题是：为什么我们更多地偏爱民主和人性化而排斥专制和粗暴的做法呢？说到这个"为什么"，我指的是我们更偏爱它们的原因，而不仅仅是那些导致我们产生这种偏爱的理由。原因之一可能在于我们不仅一直在学校接受教育，而且通过出版物、教堂、讲坛、我们的法律以及立法机构获得教育，故而民主政治是最好的社会机构。在我们的实践中，这种观念可能已经深入人心，成为了构建我们精神和道德世界司空见惯的一部分。但是，类似的理由已经导致不同环境中的另一些人产生了相当不同的观念——比如说，他们执着于法西斯主义。我们更偏爱某种事物的原因与我们为什么应该选择某种事物的理由这二者大相径庭。

在此处我并不打算去详细阐述这种原因，但是我想问一个简单的问题：民主社会的各种政策较之于非民主或者反民主的社会生活中的那些政策，更能促使人们形成好的品质，更能广泛地被人们接受和喜爱，那我们到底能否最终找到任何理由不认可这种信念呢？尊重个人自由和人类关系中的宽容和仁慈的原则，最终将使人们相信，这些原则同压制、暴力和强迫的方法相比，有助于更多的人获得更高品质的经验，难道不是这样吗？我们相信，互相协商和通过

第三章 经验的标准

说服而取得的信任，比与此相反的做法能够在在宽泛的环境下提供更高质量的经验，难道这不是我们偏爱的理由吗？

倘若对这些问题的回答是肯定的，那么崇尚进步教育的根本原因则在于其依据和运用了合乎人性的方法以及它与民主主义有着密切的关系，要是追根溯源的话也在于我们做的区分是在不同经验的内在价值之间进行的。因而，我又回到了经验的连续性原则，并把它作为这种区分的标准。

实际上，若从生物学上来解释，那么连续性原则依据的就是习惯。习惯的基本特征就是每种经验都会在实践中革新和修改自身，然而不管我们希望与否，它都会影响到以后经验的质量。凡是经历过这种经验的人，他多多少少会变得与以往有些微的不同。与普通的认为习惯是或多或少的做事的固定方法这一概念相比，这里对习惯原则的理解显然是更深入了，尽管它包括了习惯的普通概念中把习惯作为特殊情况的那一部分。习惯的原则包括态度的形成，即情感和理智态度的形成，也包括那些我们遇到并应对日常生活中发生的一切状况的基本情感和方法。从这一角度来看，经验的连续性原则意味着每种经验既会从过去的经验中获取一些东西，又会以某种方式改变以后要经历的那种经验的性质。正如诗人所描绘的那样：

一切经验就像一扇拱门，
光亮辉映着人迹未至的世尘。

> 每当我一步一步向它走近，
> 闪亮的光晕便荡然无存。
> ……

然而，到目前为止，我们还没有区分各种经验的依据。因为这一原则是普适的应用准则，所以在任何情况下都有某些连续性。只有当我们清楚经验连续性起作用的不同形式时，我们才能获得区分各种经验的基本准则。我可以通过一个以前曾经提出过却一直遭受非议的想法来阐明我的观点，即如果用现在分词"growing"（"正在生长"）一词来理解生长，那么教育过程就是生长过程。

生长或者正在发展着的生长，不仅指身体的生长，而且指理智和道德方面的生长，它是连续性原则的一个例子。然而，有人持反对的观点，他们认为，生长可能有许多不同的方向，例如，一个人刚开始从事偷盗这一行业，可能会沿着那个方向发展，经年累月，就会成为一个扒窃老手。因此，人们争辩说，仅仅有"生长"是不够的，我们必须详尽解释生长发生的方向以及其趋向的终极目的。然而，我们必须对这种情况稍做进一步分析之后，才能确定这种反对观点是否令人信服。

毋庸置疑，那样的一种人有可能生长为窃贼、歹徒或者腐败的政客。但是，从生长即教育和教育即生长这一角度来看，问题在于：通常情况下沿着这一方向的生长到底是促进还是阻碍了生长。这种

第三章 经验的标准

生长形式是为进一步的生长创造了条件，还是设置了一些障碍使以这种特殊方式生长的人失去以新的方向继续生长的诱因、刺激和机会呢？一种特殊形式的生长会对为其他方面的发展独辟蹊径的态度和习惯产生什么样的效果呢？你们可以自己来回答这些问题，这里我只想简单地说，当一种特殊方面的发展有助于继续生长的时候，也只有在这个时候，它才符合教育即生长的标准。因为概念必须具有普适性，而不是只适用于那些特殊的有限范围。

现在再来谈谈连续性问题，作为一项标准，它用于区分哪些是具有教育性的经验，哪些是错误的教育性经验。正如我们所看到的，因为每种经验通过引起某种偏爱和厌恶，从而使它比较容易或比较难去服务于这个目的，它都会更多或更少地去影响到对后来经验性质的判断，所以它在任何情况下都会有某种连续性。而且，每种经验都会在某种程度上影响到后来经验所依据的那些客观条件，例如，尽管一个学习说话的儿童拥有了一项新技能和新愿望，但是他也扩大了随后学习的外部条件。当他学习阅读时，他同样开辟了一个新环境。如果一个人想要成为教师、律师、外科医生或者股票经纪人，那么在通向其目标的途中，他需要从某种程度上确定他未来从事活动的环境。他要使自己对特定的状况更具有敏感性和适应性，相应地，对另外一些事情则不用，可是若他当初做了别的选择，那么这些事情就会相应地成为他的刺激物。

然而，当连续性原则以某种方式运用到每一种情境时，目前的经验性质就会影响到这一原则运用的方式。我们来谈谈溺爱儿童和被宠坏了的儿童这一问题。这种对儿童过于纵容的影响是连续性的。它先引起一种态度，使儿童自发地产生一种需求，希望得到能满足他未来欲望和任性的人和东西，从而让儿童能为所欲为地去索要他想要的一切，同时，它也使儿童不愿也不能去应付那些需付出努力和坚持不懈才能克服的困难。事实上，这并不矛盾，经验连续性原则可能使一个人局限于低级的发展水平，从某种意义上说，这限制了其以后的生长能力。

另一方面，倘若一种经验能激发好奇心，增强动机，树立使人克服未来一切困难的强烈愿望和目标，那么这种连续性的效果就迥乎不同了。每种经验都是一种驱动力，其价值只能靠它行进的方向来判断。作为教育者的成年人，若具有较成熟的经验，则能对年轻人的经验做出判断，反之，若自身经验较不成熟，则无法去评价年轻人的经验，因此，教育者的职责就是要明白一种经验所趋向的方向。倘若教育者不用自己较为成熟的见识来帮助年轻人组织经验的各种条件，甚至扔掉他的见识，那么拥有这种较为成熟的经验就没有意义。不考虑经验的驱动力，并且不根据它所推动的方向来判断和指导经验则意味着对经验原则本身的不忠实。这种不忠实可从两个方面来理解。其一，教育者错误地以为他本应该从他过去的经验中获得理解；其二，他也不相信所有的人类经验最终都是社会性的——包含相互接触和交往。从道德方面来理解，成熟的人没有权利抑制年轻人在既定情境下从他自己经验中获得的富有同情的理解力。

第三章 经验的标准

然而，一说到这些事情，又会趋向另一个极端，以为上面所说的只是为某种来自外部的变相的灌输做辩护。因此，值得说明的是，成年人能够增强他自己丰富的经验所赋予他的智慧，而无须强加一种单纯外力的控制。一方面，他的责任就是机警地感知哪些态度和习惯正在趋于形成。以这种趋势，倘若他是一名教育者，他必须能够判断出哪些态度确实起到了引导继续生长的作用，而哪些是阻碍继续生长的。另外，他必须对个体有富于同情的理解，能知道那些正在学习的个体头脑里正在想什么。对于家长和教师来说，在其他诸多事情当中都需具备这些能力，他们基于自己的生活经验建立教育体系，并成功地去实施它，这要比直接遵循传统的教育模式更困难一些。

但是，还有另一方面的问题。经验并不只是在个体内部进行，它一直存在着，因为它影响着愿望和目标态度的形成。然而，这并不是我要说的全部。每一种真正的经验都有积极的一面，并且在某种程度上会改变经验所处的客观条件。举一个宏观的例子来说，文明与野蛮的区别在于先前的经验已改变之后经验所处客观条件的程度。现存的道路、快速的交通运输方式、工具、器械、家具、电灯和电力都是这一类例证。如果破坏目前已文明化的经验的外部条件，那么，我们的经验就会暂时倒退到野蛮民族。

总之，从出生到死亡，我们都生活在一个人与物共存的世界之中，这个世界之所以是现在这样，是因为以前人类一直所从事的活动并且将其传递给了我们。如果我们忽视这一事实,那么经验就被当成一些似乎只在个体身心之中进行的东西。毫无疑问,经验并不是在真空中产生的,在个体之外,还有一些产生经验的源泉,它不断地为经验提供养分。没有人会质疑:贫民窟里的儿童与来自书香世家的儿童有不同的经验,乡村的儿童与城市的儿童有不同的经验,海边长大的儿童与内陆草原的儿童有不同的经验。通常情况下,我们都会想当然地以为这些太习以为常了,根本不值一提。然而,当认识到教育的意义时,我们又获得了第二种方法,即教育者不必采用强迫灌输的方式就可以对年轻人的经验给予指导。教育者的主要职责就是,他们不仅要了解到通过塑造环境条件来形成实际经验的一般原则,而且要具体地认识到哪些环境有利于获得引起生长的经验。总的来说,他们应该知道如何利用现存的自然和社会环境,并从中获取一切必需且有利于构建有价值的经验的东西。

传统教育不需要面对这样的问题,它可以有意地去避开这种责任。传统教育下,学校环境只需包括课桌、黑板、小的校园就足够了。教师不需要非常熟悉当地社区、自然、历史、经济以及职业等方面的状况,倘若只是为了利用它们作为教育资源的话。与之相反,建立在教育与经验必须相关联的基础上的教育制度,倘若要忠实于它自己的原则,则必须时时考虑这些状况。此外,进步主义教育之所以比以往的传统教育更难以实施,还在于增加到教育者身上的负担。

在制订教育计划时,有意地使客观条件迎合正在受教育的个体,

第三章 经验的标准

这是有可能的。无论何时,只要让教师、书本、仪器设备以及每一样能代表年长者更成熟经验的产品等的地位和作用,有意地从属于儿童当时的倾向和情感,那么,这种情况就起作用了。任何理论,只要认为这些客观条件是重要的,都只是以施加外力控制并限制个体自由为代价的,它就最终总是基于这种观念,即只有当客观条件从属于有经验的个体的内心状况时,这种经验才能称为真正的经验。

我并不是说客观条件可以被摒除,只是认为它们必须融合于并参与到我们生活的世界里,这是个人与物共存的世界,所以对客观条件做出如此多的让步就是不可避免的事实。但是,我认为,对一些家庭和学校所从事的活动进行持续的观察,就会发现一些家长和教师在行事时会遵循使客观条件从属于内心这一想法。在那种情况下,可以假设不仅内心的想法是主要的,从某种意义上说也确实是主要的,而且只要它们暂时存在着,它们就适合整个教育过程。

让我用一个婴儿的例子来加以阐述。从某一个方面来讲,婴儿对食物、休息以及活动的需要当然是主要的、有决定意义的。要给婴儿提供营养;要保证其有舒适的睡眠,等等。但是,这些事实并不意味着,只要孩子吵闹或者发怒,父母就要随时喂他,也并不意味着没有固定的喂奶和睡眠时间等。有智慧的母亲往往会考虑婴儿的需要,调节客观条件,满足婴儿的需求,而不是去推卸自己的责任。如果在这方面她是一位有智慧的母亲,她就不仅会利用专家提供的经验,而且会利用自己的经验去筛选,在通常情况下哪些经验有益于婴儿的正常发育。她并不是使这些客观条件从属于婴儿当下的内部状态，而是对其做出了有条理的整合，以便与婴儿当下的内部状态发生特殊的交互作用。

我一直使用"交互作用"（interaction）这个词，在于它体现了经验的第二个主要原则，主要用来解释经验的教育作用和力量。这一原则赋予经验的客观条件和主观条件这两个因素同等的权利，任何正常的经验都是这两种条件的交互作用。这两种条件被放在一起，或者在它们的交互作用中，它们便形成了我们所说的"情境"（situation）。传统教育的问题不在于它强调进入经验控制的外部条件，而在于它很少关注内在因素，而恰恰是这种内部因素决定了获得哪种经验。从这一方面来看，传统教育违背了交互作用这一原则，但是，除非新教育以前面提到的极端的非此即彼的教育哲学为依据，否则，它不能以此为理由从另一方面违背这个原则。

这种需要调节婴儿发展的客观条件的例子说明了：第一，父母有责任来安排婴儿获得饮食、睡眠等经验的种种条件；第二，这种责任是利用过去积累的经验来完成的，比如说，借鉴一些称职的医生和那些对正常身体生长有特殊研究的研究者的建议。当母亲运用这些知识去调节婴儿营养和睡眠的客观条件时，她的自由是否会受到限制呢？或者说，这是否增强了母亲承担父母职责的智慧，从而拓宽了她的自由呢？毫无疑问，若盲目地迷信这种建议和指导，以至在任何可能的状况下都一成不变地遵循这些指令，那么这就限制了父母和儿童的自由。但是，这种限制也是该智慧在个人判断中运用的局限性。

调节客观条件会在哪些方面限制婴儿的自由呢？当一个婴儿想继续玩耍却被放到婴儿车里时，或者当婴儿饿了却不给他食物时，再或者当婴儿因想得到照料而哭泣却没有人抱他、爱抚他时，婴儿当时的行为和情感确实就受到了某些限制。当婴儿即将跌进火堆，恰好被母亲或保姆急忙拉开时，这也是一种限制。随后，我将会花更多的篇幅来谈谈自由。此处，我只问问以下问题就够了：我们对自由的定义到底是基于一些相对的暂时的偶然事件来考虑和判断，还是在发展经验的连续性过程中得以发现呢？

具体来说，个体生活在世界里的说法，意味着个人生活在一系列的情境里。当人们说到他们生活在这些情境里时，"在……里"（in）的意思与它在所谓的"钱在口袋里"或者"油漆在漆桶里"的意思是不同的。进一步来讲，它意味着交互作用是在个体与客体以及其他人之间进行的。情境和交互作用的概念是彼此不可分割的。经验总是个体与形成他的环境之间发生交互作用的产物，不管这个环境是否由与他讨论话题或事件的人，或者由他讨论的有关部分情境的话题，或者由他玩的玩具，或者由他正在读的书（此时，他的环境条件可能是英国、希腊或某一想象的地区），又或者由他正在做的实验所用的材料等组成。换句话说，环境就是指与个人需要、愿望、目的及能力等发生作用以产生经验的所有条件，甚至当一个人在幻想建一个空中楼阁时，他也是在与他幻想的建造物之间发生交互作用。

连续性和交互作用这两个原则之间彼此是密不可分的，它们纵横交错、环环相扣，也可以说，它们是构成经验的纵横两方面。不同的情境依次一个接一个地产生。但是，由于这个连续性原则，之前情境中的某些东西会被传递到之后的情境当中。当一个人从一种情境进入另一种情境时，他的世界、他的环境不是扩大了就是缩小了，他并不会认为他生活在另一个世界，而只是生活在同一世界的不同部分或方面而已。在一种情境中他所学的知识和技能方面的东西，会成为有效地理解和处理后来情境的工具，其过程会随着生活和学习的持续而不断往前推进。否则，因产生经验的各个因素是分离的，故经验的过程也会是杂乱无章的。一个分裂的世界，一个各个部分和方面都四分五裂的世界，会即刻成为一个人人格分裂的迹象和起因。当这种分裂达到了某个临界点时，我们就称这个人为疯子。另一方面，只有当相继出现的经验首尾相连、彼此结合时，一个完满的人格才能最终形成。也只有当建立一个各个事物彼此相连的世界时，才能形成完满的人格。

连续性和交互作用彼此积极地结合在一起，这就可以用来衡量经验的教育意义和价值。故而，一个教育者当前直接关心的事情就是交互作用发生的情境。因素之一就是在特定时间里参与到交互作用中的个人，另一个因素就是全部的客观条件，它们在某种程度上会受到教育者的调节。正如上面已经解释过的那样，"客观条件"这一术语的含义很宽泛，它包括教育者所做的事情和处事的方法，不仅包括其所说的话，而且包括说话时的语调。它亦包括设备、书籍、仪器、玩具以及游戏。它包括个体参与交互作用的材料，最重要的是，它包括个体所参与构建的整个社会情境。

当我们说到客观条件是指在教育者的权力内可以调节的那些方面时，当然，它的意思就是指教育者有能力去直接影响别人的经验，并且直接影响到他们受到的教育，这让他肩负起决定环境的责任，这种环境与受教育者当下的能力和需要交互作用，从而创造有价值的经验。传统教育的弊端不在于教育者自己担负起了提供环境的责任，而在于他们在催生经验时没有考虑到另一个因素，即受教育者的能力和目的。他们认为，某一类客观条件即使不能唤起个体对某事物的反应能力，其本身也是值得被期待的。缺乏相互适应使得教学和学习过程充满了偶然性。一些人，若给他们提供客观条件，他们就能顺利地进行学习，而另一些人则会尽自己的最大所能来学习。选择客观条件的责任，是与理解在既定时间内从事学习的个体的需要和能力的责任息息相关的。在其他时候用在其他个体身上的某些材料和方法已经被证明是有效的，这还是不够的。一定要考虑到，它们将会在产生一种在特殊的时间对特殊的个体具有教育性质的经验时发挥作用才行。

不给婴儿吃牛排，并不是说牛排不具有营养价值。在小学里，不教一年级至五年级的学生三角学课程，并不是说它让人感到厌恶。

具有教育意义或者引导经验生长的并不在于学科本身。若不考虑学习者达到的生长阶段，那就没有任何科目内部或本身具有固有的教育价值。正是没有考虑满足个体的能力和需要才催生了这样的观念，即某些科目和某些方法有内在的文化价值，或者对心智的训练有内在的好处。不存在所谓抽象的教育价值。传统教育之所以缩减了如此多的教育材料，并使之变成了预先消化过的知识，其原因就在于其相信掌握某些科目和方法，加上熟知某些事实和真相，这本身就具有教育价值。基于这种观念，只要按照所用教材的数量和难度，逐级分类，然后制订出月计划和年计划就足够了。不然的话，就是期待学生去接受外部规定的所有内容。倘若学生对其置之不理、不接受它，或者学生直接旷课或心不在焉，甚至最后对该门课程产生反感的情绪，则被认为是犯了错误。至于这种问题是否可能由教材本身或者教学方法造成，就不去质疑了。交互作用的原则清晰地表明：若教材不适应个体的需要和能力，就可能使经验丧失教育作用，同样地，若个体不能使自己适应教材，也会使经验丧失教育作用。

然而，在教育实践中，连续性原则是指在教育过程的每一个阶段，我们都要考虑到未来的状况。在传统教育下，这种观念很容易被误解，甚至会受到严重的曲解。传统教育认为，学生获得某些技能、学会某些其后来（也许在大学里或在成人生活中）需要的学科知识，事实上都是在为其未来的需要和环境做准备。当今"准备"是一个让人雾里看花的观念。从某种意义上讲，每种经验都应提供某些借鉴，使人能做好准备去获取之后更深刻、更广泛的经验。这就是经验的生长、经验的连续性和经验的改造的含义。但是，如果认为，仅仅因为可能在未来的某个时候有用，而去教授或学习一些算术、地理、历史等方面的知识，那么这种理解就是错误的；如果认为，在某种情况下获得的一些阅读技能和计算技能，在相当不同的情况下，也将会自然而然地做好正确而有效地运用它们的准备，那么这种理解也是错误的。

几乎每一个人都曾偶尔回想起他学生时代的日子，他想知道求学期间他学到的那些知识究竟产生了什么样的效果，而且，他也想知道，为什么他已经学会的那些技巧和能力，在改变了形式之后，还需要重新学习，他才能很好地驾驭。确实，若一个人认为如果只是为了取得进步、为了智慧上的继续提高，过去在学校里学得的知识就已经足够了，而不必重新学习更多的知识，那么他真的很幸运。这并不是说他没有把功课学好，只是因为其在求学时期已经学过该知识，并且已经顺利通过了考试。问题之一在于其过去学习的教材是孤立的，这就好像把知识放进了不透水的船舱里一样。那么，这些知识的效果如何？知识到哪里去了呢？正确的答案就是：知识仍然储存在原来存放它们的密闭的船舱里面。如果当初学习知识时的情境再次出现，那么，这些知识就会被重新唤起，并且能发挥其作用。但是，当初学习这些知识时，它们还是相互孤立的，因此，它们与其他的经验并没有很密切的联系，故而在实际生活情境当中并没有多大用处。经验的规律表明：不管当时的学习多么精深，它都应该产生真正的准备作用，而此处的这类学习违背了这种规律。

关于准备的说法，其缺欠还不仅表现在上面这一点上。一种观念认为，也许教育学上最大的错误在于，一个人所学的知识只是他当初学到的特定的东西而已。附带学习（collateral learning），作为一种能够形成忍耐态度、个人好恶的学习方式，可能而且往往要比拼写课、地理课或历史课的学习重要得多，因为这些态度是未来学习的根基。最重要的态度就是能够促使学习者产生继续学习的强烈渴望。倘若这方面的动机减弱而不是增强，那就会发生比仅仅缺乏准备更为严重的事情。事实上，学生的天赋能力就被剥夺了，不然的话，这些能力就能助他应付他生命历程中遇到的各种状况。我们时常会遇到一些人，他们几乎没有受过学校教育，而恰恰是这种缺少教育的情况，促成他们形成了积极的态度。他们至少还保持着基本的常识和判断力，并把常识和判断力运用到实际生活情境中，这使他们具有了从已有经验中学习的宝贵能力品质。倘若在此过程中，个体丧失了自己的灵魂、丧失了对与此相关的重要事物的评判能力，如果他丧失了渴望去运用他所学知识的愿望，更重要的是，他丧失了从即将出现的未来经验中吸取精华的能力，那么，学习那些事先编订的地理和历史知识、获得读写能力又有何用呢？

那么，在教育计划中，准备的真正含义是什么呢？首先，它是指一个人，青年人或者老年人，从他当下的经验中获得以后要用时对其有用的一切东西。如果准备成了控制的目的，那就会因一个虚拟的未来而牺牲了当下的诸多潜能。当这样做时，就误解或歪曲了为未来做准备的真正含义。认为利用现在仅仅是为未来做准备这一观念本身也是自相矛盾的，它忽视了甚至根本否认了一个人之所以能为未来做好准备，恰恰是因为目前这些经验条件。我们总是生活在当下，而不是别的某个时候，而且只有当从每一个当前的经验中吸取其全部意义时，我们才是在为未来做相同的事情做好准备。归根结底，对任何事情来说，这才是唯一的准备。

总之，之前所说的意思是，我们应该周密地考虑经验产生的各种条件，只有在这些条件下，所有当前的经验才具有有价值的意义。不要认为当前的经验是什么都无关紧要，只要它能令人满意就行了，结果恰恰与此相反，而且，这也是很容易从一个极端走向另一个极端的事情。因为传统教育往往倾向于为了那个遥远且虚无缥缈的未来而去牺牲现在，所以它认为教育者不必为年轻人正在经历的这种当前的经验负责任。然而，现在与未来并不是一种非此即彼的关系，无论如何，现在都会影响未来。对这两者的关系有些了解的人就是那些已经成熟的人。因而，他们有责任去构建对未来产生有益影响的当前经验的各种条件。教育，即生长或成熟，应该是一个永久现时的过程。

第四章　社会的控制

我曾经说过，用生活的经验来看待教育，其计划和设计就要构建和采纳一种明智的理论，如果你觉得合适，可称之为经验的哲学。否则，教育就会完全被一次次吹来的学术之风所摆布。我曾提请大家注意构成经验的两条基本原则，以便说明这种理论的必要性。这两条原则是交互作用和连续性。如果有人问我，为什么要花费那么多的时间，去详细论述一种相当抽象的哲学，这是因为试图用教育以生活经验为基础的观念作为建立学校的基础，实践中必然会出现一些矛盾和混乱，除非在尝试之前了解什么是经验，并且把教育性经验与非教育性经验以及错误的教育经验区别开来。现在，我开始讨论一些实际的教育问题，相信这些讨论会提供比先前更为具体的话题和素材。

连续性和交互作用这两条原则作为衡量经验价值的标准，紧密相关，我们很难说清楚哪个特定的教育问题是最先出现的。即使是用最简便的方式把教材或各门学科以及教和学的方法问题划分开来，也不能帮助我们选择和组织讨论的主题。所以，在决定讨论主题从哪里开始和其先后顺序时，多少带有一些随意性。不管怎样，我还是应该从个人自由和社会控制这些老问题开始，进而讨论由此而生的一些问题。

考虑教育上的问题，一开始暂时忽略学校问题，而先思考其他的人类的情境，这样做往往很好。我觉得没有一个人会否认，普通的好公民，在事实上是更容易受社会控制的，而且其中的大部分控制并不会让人感觉对个人自由会产生束缚。甚至那种思想上信奉无政府主义的人，其哲学观念认为国家的或政府的控制是十足有害的事，而他却相信，在废除国家的政治统治之后，其他形式的社会控制也会发挥作用。实际上，他对政治管理的抗议源于自身的信念，即在废除国家统治的同时，会有其他更加完善的控制模式来发挥作用。

我们要撇开这种极端的立场，关注在日常生活中发挥作用的社会控制的实例，寻求其背后的基本原则。让我们从儿童本身开始讨论。儿童在休息时或在课后做游戏，从"捉人游戏""一只老猫"到打棒球和踢足球，这些游戏中都有规则，这些规则指导着儿童的行为。这些游戏不是随意进行的，也不是由临时起意的一连串动作组成的。没有规则就没有游戏。如果有了争论，那就由一位裁判员来评定，或者用讨论和仲裁的方法去解决；否则，这场游戏就将被破坏，就此终止。

第四章 社会的控制

在这些情况中,我希望大家能够注意到一些非常明显的控制性特征。第一,规则是游戏的组成部分,并不是游戏之外的东西。没有规则,也就没有游戏了;规则不同,游戏也就不一样。只要游戏合理而顺利地进行着,那么做游戏的人就不会感到他们正在服从外来的强制约束,而是觉得自己正在玩一个游戏。第二,有人可能觉得一种评判是不公平的,也许甚至为此而大动肝火。但是,他并不是反对规则,而是反对违反规则的行为,反对偏向一方和不公正的行动。第三,这些规则是完全标准化的,因此,用规则来指导的游戏也是完全标准化的。凡属计分、选择场地的哪一边、占据什么位置以及规定动作,等等,都有一些公认的方式。这些规则是由传统和先例所认可的。或者,那些做游戏的人看过专业性比赛,想要模仿比他们年长的人。一种约定俗成的惯例因素是非常牢固的。一般说来,只有看到模仿的成年队改变了规则之后,少年队才会改变自己的游戏规则,因为由年长者做出的改变,至少应该可以使游戏更加富有技巧性或更具观赏性。

现在,我得出的普遍结论是个人行为的控制受到其所处整体情境的影响。在整个情境中,人们共同参与活动,他们是合作者或者是发生交互作用的各个部分。因为即使在竞争性游戏中,也是某种形式的参与和共享经验的过程。换句话说,那些参加游戏的人并不觉得自己是在受某一个人的指挥,或者在遵照某些场外上司的意愿行事。激烈争论往往是由于裁判员或有些人不公平地偏袒一方;换句话说,在这些场合下,有些人企图把他的个人意愿强加给别人。

用这个实例来论证社会控制个人的普遍原则并不侵犯自由，似乎有点小题大做。但是，我认为，如果能通过更多的案例来说明此理，那么这个从特殊到一般的结论就是站得住脚的。游戏大都具有竞争性。如果我们举出小组的所有成员都要参加的合作性活动的例子，比如说，在一个秩序完善的家庭中生活的成员之间相互信赖，那么这个论点就会更加清楚了。在所有这些情况下，不是按照任何个人的意愿和期望来建立秩序，而是依靠全体成员的活动精神。这种控制是社会性的，但是，个人是社会的一个部分，而不是在社会之外。

我并不是说，在上述的情况下没有施展权威的机会，父母不必介入，不需要实施相对直接的控制。可是，我要说，第一，与在所有的人都参与活动的情况下所实施的控制相比，在家庭中直接控制的机会要少一些。而且更为重要的是，在一个管理有序的家庭或其他社会团体中，权威的施展并不仅仅是个人意愿的表现；父母或教师是作为整个团体利益的代表者和代理人来施展权威的。对于这一点，在一个秩序完备的学校里，对这个人或那个人的控制，主要是依靠各种活动和维护这些活动的情境。教师要把以个人方式施展权威的机会减少到最低限度。第二，有必要时言行要坚定，那也是为了团体的利益，而不是为了显示个人的权力。武断任意的行动和公平合理的行动之间的区别也就在于此。

此外，为了使人们在经验中体会到这种区别，并不需要由教师或儿童用语言表达出来。极少数儿童不能清晰地分辨由个人权力和欲望引起的行动与公正的、符合所有人的利益的行动（虽然他们不能用语言说清楚，但至少能遵照这种理智原则）。我甚至愿意这样说，总体而言，儿童比成年人更容易体察这种区别的一些征兆和表现。当儿童与别人一起做游戏时，就能学会区分。如果某个孩子的行动能够增加所做事情的经验的价值，那么其他孩子就愿意，而且往往特别愿意接受这个孩子的建议，让他做孩子王。然而，他们却很讨厌这个孩子指手画脚的举动。最终孩子们常常不欢而散，问及原因，他们便说，照那样干"太霸道了"。

我并不想用讽刺的方法挖苦传统学校，而是要反映其真实情景。但是，我认为有一种说法是公正的，即在传统学校里教师往往过度使用个人命令，学校里的秩序是对成人意愿的彻底服从，这是由于传统学校的情境几乎迫使教师不得不这么做。传统学校不是由人们共同参与活动而结合起来的小组或团体。因此，它缺少正常的合适的控制条件。为了弥补这个不足，在很大程度上就不得不依靠教师的直接干涉，即通常所谓的"维持秩序"。教师能够维持秩序，是因为教师有维持秩序的职责，而不是因为秩序存在于共同参与的活动中。

我们得出的结论是：在所谓的新学校里，社会控制主要源于作为社会事业的工作本质之中，在这项工作中，每个人都有机会且感觉有义务为此做出贡献。大多数儿童天生就是"爱好交际的"。他们甚至比成年人更加厌恶孤独。真正的团体生活是以天生的社交性为基础的。但是团体生活本身又不能完全自发地、持久地组织起来。

它要求预先思考和计划。教育者应该懂得有关个人的知识，懂得有关教材的知识，这些知识有助于为社会组织选择有益的活动。在这种社会组织中，每个人都有机会做出某种贡献，并且，在这种社会组织中，全体人员都参与的活动是控制的主要手段。

对于儿童，我并不是那么想入非非，认为每个学生都能尽其责，或者任何一个有正常强烈冲动的儿童在每个场合中都能尽其责。可能有一些儿童，当他们进入学校时，在校外已经受到了不利条件的伤害，并且变得相当被动和过分顺从，以至不能做出什么贡献。也有另外一些儿童，先前的经验使他们成为盲目自大和任性不羁的人，或者成为锋芒外露的反叛者。但是，可以肯定的是，不能根据这些情况来预测社会控制的普遍原则。当然，也找不到可以对付这些情况的普遍原则。教师必须对这些儿童进行个别教育。虽然可以将这些儿童笼统地归为一类，但是没有两个人是完全一样的。教师（男教师或女教师）要尽其所能地找出造成这些顽抗态度的原因。如果要使教育过程继续进行下去，那么教师就不能造成一种局面，使一种意志对抗另一种意志来验证哪种意志是最为强大的，也不能容许那些任性的、不参加活动的学生一直影响其他人的教育活动。在某些时候，拒绝他们参加活动也许是唯一可行的手段，但是，这样做并没有解决问题。因为这样做可能会使那些儿童反社会的态度（例如想出风头和炫耀逞能等令人讨厌的行为）愈演愈烈。

这些例外的情况很难证明一个规则，也很难提供一些线索来证明如何制定一个规则。因此，我不会过多地强调这些例外情况的重要性，虽然现在进步学校确实经常出现这种超出常规的事件，因为家长可能把进入这样的学校作为儿童教育最后的无奈手段。我认为，进步学校在控制上的欠缺并不是源自任何一个特殊事件。这种欠缺很有可能是由于未能预先安排这种工作（我指的是参与其间的各种活动）。这种工作可以创造一些情境，情境本身能够控制这个学生、那个学生或其他学生要做些什么和怎样去做。缺少预先安排，往往是由于缺少充分考虑的前期计划。有多种原因会导致这种缺陷。应当指出，其中一个特别重要的原因与一种观念有关，即认为这种预先的计划是不必要的，甚至认为这样做本来就违反了他们所倡导的真正的自由。

当然，由教师预先做出的计划很可能是相当呆板严格的，而且在理智上不具有灵活性。这种计划是由成年人强迫执行的，尽管在实施时运用了老练机敏的手段，并且在表面上尊重了个人的自由，但这种计划依然是外在的东西。这种计划没有遵从所需要的原则。只有当教师能够安排有助于团体活动的种种条件，而且这些条件有助于一种组织运行，这种组织借助于所有的人都要参与共同计划的事实来控制个人的冲动时，他们才能体现出自己较为成熟的一面，并且让自身关于世界、教材和个人的广博知识发挥作用。这种预先做出的计划，如同惯例一样，实行起来几乎没有给个人留下思考的余地，或者，也不能使具有特长的人找到用武之地，可是，不能因此就否定一切计划。相反，教育者要义不容辞地制定一种更明智的，因而也更困难的计划。他必须对接受教育的特定个体进行仔细的调查，包括其能力和需求，同时，为了让学生获取经验，必须安排各种情境来提供教材或内容，以便满足他们的各种需要和发展他们的各项能力。这种计划必须具有一定的灵活性，让经验的个体性得以尽情展现，同时又必须具有相当的稳定性，为能力的后续发展提供明确的指引。

现在我们有个适当的机会来谈论有关教师的职责和任务了。经验是通过交互作用得以发展的这一条原理意味着：教育实质上是一种社会化的过程。这种社会化的程度，取决于个人组成社会团体的程度。把教师排斥到这个团体之外，是一件荒谬的事情。因为教师是这一团体中最成熟的成员，他对社会团体生活中最重要的各种交往和相互交流负有特定的引导责任。儿童的个人自由应当得到尊重，而更成熟的人却要被剥夺个人自由——这种观点极为荒谬，是不值一驳的。教师是团体中的一分子，而排斥其在团体活动中的积极的指导作用——这种趋势是从一个极端走向另一个极端的又一个事例。当学生们组成一个班级，而不是组成一个社会团体时，教师肯定大都是从外部发挥作用的，而不是作为人人都参与的交换过程的指导者。当教育是以经验作为基础时，教育经验即可被视为一种社会化的过程，这种情况就发生了根本的变化。教师失去了外部的监督者或独裁者的地位，而成为团体活动的领导者。

在将游戏的指导作为正常的社会控制的例子进行讨论时，我曾经提到存在着标准化的惯例因素。在学校生活中也可以发现类似的

第四章 社会的控制

因素,即言谈举止的问题,尤其是体现文明礼仪的优雅行为。我们对世界各个不同地区在人类历史上不同时代的风俗习惯知道得越多,就越能了解风俗习惯是因时因地而异的。这个事实证明有大量的惯例因素存在。在任何时代或任何地方,没有一个团体没有风俗习惯的规则,例如恰当的问候方式。特定的惯例没有什么是固定的和绝对的。但是,某些形式的惯例的实质并不在于惯例本身。惯例是一切社会关系都同样具有的伴随物,至少,它是防止或减少社会摩擦的滑润油。

当然,这些社会的形式也可能会变为我们所说的"徒具外表",变成没有内在意义的表面形式。但是,避免社会交往中的空洞的形式主义,并不意味着反对任何形式的要素。说得更恰当一点儿,它是表明需要建立本身就适合社会情境的一些交往形式。人们去某些进步学校参观,为偶尔碰到一些不讲礼貌的事情而感到惊奇;了解情况的人则比较清楚,这种不礼貌的行为在某种程度上是由于儿童热衷于他们正在进行的工作。例如,在他们兴致勃勃地热衷于自己的工作时,可能彼此会发生碰撞,甚至撞到了参观者,却没有说一句道歉的话。有人可能会说,这种情况比起那种单纯拘泥于外在形式而缺乏理智上的和情感上的兴趣,还是要好一些的。但是,缺乏礼貌也是教育工作上的一种失败,这是没有学到人生中最为重要的功课:相互磨合与适应。如果在教育过程中形成的各种态度和习惯妨碍未来的学习,那么这种教育便是片面的,因为未来的学习源自与他人的便利可行的接触和交流。

第五章　自由的性质

关于社会控制问题的另一个方面，即关于自由的本质，我想不厌其烦地再讲一些意见。只有理智的自由才是唯一永远重要的自由，也就是说，它是基于真正的内在价值这一目的，能够做出观察和判断的自由。我想，关于自由问题出现的最普遍的错误是，把自由认定为活动的自由，或认定为外部的或身体方面的活动。可是，这种外部的和身体方面的活动又不能与内部方面的活动相分离，不能与思想、愿望和目的自由分开。在典型的传统学校的教室里，课桌椅固定排列和对学生采取军事化管理，只准学生听从某种固定的信号活动，这种对外部活动加以限制的做法，实际上也是对理智自由和道德自由的极大限制。必须把如同囚衣和镣铐之类的程序全部废除，个人才能通过智力上的自由得到生长的机会。没有这种自由，就不能保证真正的可持续的常态发展。

但是，仍然存在着这样的事实，即增加外部活动自由的措施只是一种手段，而不是一种目的。即使获得了外部活动的自由，教育上的问题也并未解决。就教育问题而言,任何事情都取决于利用这种新增的自由去做什么、为了什么目的去做、将带来什么后果。让我们首先来说说增加外部自由可能带来的好处。第一,对教师来说,若是没有外部的自由,实际上不可能获得个人所关注的知识。强迫之下的安静和默许让学生无法展示自己的天性,只会形成虚假的一致性。他们注重表面形式,认为形式在实质之先。他们鼓励保持注意、礼节和服从等外部的表面形式。在盛行这种制度的学校里,每个对此熟悉的人都十分了解,在这种表象的背后,都不知不觉地充斥着各种思想、想象、欲望和心照不宣的活动。只是当某些不正常的行为露出马脚时,教师才能察觉出这些表象背后的东西。一个人只要把这种非常虚假的情况与学校以外的正常的人际关系,比如与完美的家庭关系进行对比,就会感觉到教师熟悉和理解那些作为受教育者的个人是多么重要的事。而如果没有这种洞察力,要使个人真正地理解教学中使用的教材和方法,并且使其在个人心灵和品格的发展中发挥实际作用,恐怕就要碰运气了。这里存在着一种恶性的循环。教材和教法的机械的一致性,造成了一种始终如一的固定性,这种固定性反过来又造成了刻板守成的学习和背诵,在其背后一些个人的倾向就以非常规的、或多或少被禁止的方式表现出来。

增加外部自由的另一个重要好处表现在学习过程的本质上。如前所述,比较陈旧的方法注重被动性和接受性。这些特征特别强调束缚身体的活动。在标准化的学校中,只有不正常的或者反抗的活动才能摆脱这种情况。在实验室或车间里是不可能完全安静的。传

第五章 自由的性质

统学校把宁静标榜为一种首要的美德，这个事实表明了传统学校的非社会性质。当然，的确也存在高强度的智力活动并不包含明显的身体活动这样的情况。但是如果长时间地继续下去，就会发现这种智力活动的效能要发挥出来需要一个漫长的过程。甚至对于儿童来说，也应当有短暂的时间用来做沉静的反思。但是，只有经历了多次外显活动之后，才需要时间进行真正的反思，将在这些无须动脑只要动手和动身体的活动中的收获进行整理。活动的自由也是一种保持身心健康的重要手段。我们仍然需要学习希腊人的榜样，他们很了解健全的身体和健全的精神之间的关系。但是从上面提到的各个方面来看，外部活动的自由只是获得自由的一种手段，借此可以获得判断的自由和将精心选择的目标贯彻执行的权力上的自由。需要有多少外部自由，这是因人而异的。这种需求会随着成熟而减少。不过，如果完全没有这种外部的自由，即使是一个足够成熟的个人，也很难接触到那些能够促进其智力发展的新材料。这种自由活动的数量和质量是成长的一种手段，这是教育者在每个发展阶段中都必须加以考虑的问题。

然而，把这种自由本身当作一种目的，乃是最大的错误。这样，就有可能会破坏作为正常秩序源泉的共同参与的合作活动。可是，从另一方面来看，这样又能把本应是积极的自由转化为某种消极的东西。自由若不加以限制，便走向了消极方面，其价值仅仅在于作为一种手段去取得力量，即：确定目的的力量，做出明智判断的力量，根据欲望所产生的行为结果来评价欲望的力量；选择和安排实践所选择的目的的力量；等等。

在任何情况下，自然的冲动和欲望都是一种起点。如果对冲动和欲望不加以某些重构、某些改造，只保持本身原有的形式，就不会有智力的生长。这种改造就包含着禁止冲动停留在最初状态。外部强制禁止的另一种方式是通过个人的反思和判断达到目的。古语说"行而后思"（stop and think）就是一种合理的心理学解释。因为思考能使冲动的即时表现停顿下来，直到那种冲动与其他可能的行动趋势发生联结，从而形成更全面、更有条理的活动计划。其他一些活动趋势是用眼、用耳和动手去观察客观条件；还有一些则是回忆过去所发生的事情。因此，思考就是推迟即时的活动，它能通过观察和记忆的联合去影响冲动的内部控制，而这种联合乃是反思的核心。这些说法可以用来解释众所周知的"自我控制"（self-control）的意义。教育的理想的目的是创造自我控制的力量。但是，单纯撤除外部的控制不能保证产生自我控制。"才离龙潭，又入虎穴"（jump out of the frying-pan into the fire）的事是很容易发生的。换句话说，逃避一种外部控制的形式，而使自己陷入另一种更危险的外部控制的形式，是很容易发生的事。冲动和欲望如果不按理智去安排就要被偶然的情境控制。摆脱别人的控制，而听任心血来潮的念头和反复无常的想法支配自己的行为，即完全由冲动摆布而无理智的判断，这样做是有百害而无一利的。如果一个人这样来控制自己的行为，那就只不过是一种自由的错觉。实际上，他的行为是不受自己控制的。

第六章　目的的意义

这样看来，把自由作为一种力量来确立目的并且落实此目的，是一种合理的天性。这种自由与自我控制是一样的，因为确立目的和组织落实目的的方法都是理智的工作。柏拉图曾经把奴隶说成实施别人目的的人。如他所说，一个人受自己盲目的欲望所支配，也会变成奴隶。我觉得，在进步教育中应该强调学习者参与确立目的，用来指导他在学习过程中的活动，没有比这种观点更恰当的了。同样，传统教育难以保证学生在确立其学习目的时积极合作，也没有比这种缺点更糟糕的了。但是，目的和结果的意义，本身是不明显的，而且从其本身也无法解释。愈是强调目的和结果在教育上的重要性，那么，了解目的是什么、它是怎样提出的以及它如何在经验中发挥作用，就愈加显得重要。

一种真正的目的往往是由冲动引发的。一种冲动受到抑制不能立即实现，就会转化为欲望。可是，冲动和欲望这两者本身都不是目的。目的本身是从结果来加以认识的。这就是说，目的包含了预见冲动之后的行动结果。这种预见中纳入了理智的作用。第一，它要求对客观条件和情境进行观察。因为冲动和欲望本身不能产生结果，而要通过它们与周围条件的交互作用或合作才能产生结果。像走路这类简单活动的冲动，只有依靠它与一个人所站立的地面发生积极有效的联结才能得以实现。一般情况下，我们没有必要过多地注意地面的情况。可是，当处于难以应付的情境时，比方说，爬一座陡峭的、崎岖不平的山，而那里又没有现成的路可走，在这种情况下，我们就必须非常仔细地观察那里的各种情况。这样看来，观察是把冲动转变为目的的一个条件。比如，当我们看到铁路交叉路口旁边的标志时，必须做到一停、二看、三听。

但是，单凭观察还是不够的。我们还必须理解所见到、所听到和所接触的事物的意义。这种意义是由按照所见到的情况去行动从而产生的结果形成的。一个婴儿可能看到火焰的亮光，便想伸手去摸它。当碰到火焰时便产生了后果，那时，他便理解到火焰的意义并不在于它的亮光，而在于燃烧的力量。我们之所以能认识到一些结果，只是由于先前的种种经验。对于我们熟悉的一些事情，因为有许多过去的经验，所以我们不必停顿下来去回想这些经验究竟是什么。我们不必特意去考虑先前的热和燃烧的经验，就能明了火焰具有光和热的意义。但是，对于一些不熟悉的事情，除非我们回顾并且反思心中的过往经验，比较它们与现实的情况有哪些相似之处，然后对现实情境做出预期的判断，否则，我们便无法预见观察到的情况到底会产生什么结果。

第六章　目的的意义

目的的形成是一个相当复杂的理智活动。其作用包括：(1) 观察周围的种种情况。(2) 熟悉过去在相似情境中发生的情况。获得这种知识的途径，有时是回忆，有时是由那些前期经验相对丰富的人提供信息、建议和警告。(3) 把观察和回忆的东西结合起来，明了它们的意义，从而做出判断。目的与原始的冲动和欲望是不同的。这是对依据特定的方式和观察到的特定的条件行动的结果做出预测，并将此转化成一种计划和行动的策略。"愿望不等于现实"。对某些东西，人们可能会产生强烈的欲望。这种欲望非常强烈，使得人们可能对此产生的行动后果弃而不顾。这类事件不能作为教育的典型范例。具有重要意义的教育问题是，在做出观察和判断之前，延缓做出以欲望为基础的即时行动。如果我没有被误解，那么这一点和进步学校的管理肯定是有关联的。过分地强调把活动作为目的，而不是强调理智的活动，就会导致将冲动和欲望的立即执行误认为自由。人们之所以信服这种看法，是因为他们混淆了冲动和目的。如上所说，除非预见到把冲动付诸实施所产生的后果，否则就延缓做出明显的活动，如果不这样，就不会有目的可言——而没有观察、知识和判断，就不可能有这种预见性。当然，单凭预见，即使是极为精准的预言，也是不够的。理智的预测和后果的观念必须与欲望和冲动结合起来，才能获得前行的力量。这也为另外那些盲目的活动指明了方向，欲望给观念提供了原动力和能量。这样一来，一种观念就可以成为可行的计划。假使一个人有一种欲望要建立一个新家，即要建造一所房子，不论他的欲望多么强烈，都不能马上变成现实。这个人必须形成一种观念，即他想要哪一种房子，包括房间的数目和布局，等等。他必须拟订一个计划，确定蓝图和规格。如果他没有清算自己有多少家底，那么这一切可能会变成消磨时间的空想娱乐。他必须考虑他的资金和可以获得的贷款与实施这个计划的关系。他必须研究是否有宅基地、价格多少、周边配套商圈是否便利、和睦相处的邻里、学校的配置，等等。所有这些事情都要慎重考虑：他的支付能力、家舍的大小和种种需求、可能的位置等，都是客观的事实。这些事实不是最初欲望里的成分，但是必须看到这些事实，并据此做出判断，以便使欲望能够转化为目的，并使目的转化为一种行动的计划。

只要不是医学上所说的感知觉完全失灵的人，每一个人就都有欲望。这些欲望是行动的首要的动力源泉。内行的商人希望事业有成；将军希望打胜仗；父母希望家居舒适，教育好孩子……此类欲望是不胜枚举的。欲望的强度可以衡量出其所付出努力的强度。但是，如果不把欲望变成可以实现的方法，那么种种希望就会成为空中楼阁。问题在于如何尽快将方法取代设计出来的想象的目的。因为方法是客观的，如果要形成一种真正的目的，就必须研究和理解种种客观的方法。

传统教育往往会忽视作为动力源泉的个人的冲动和欲望的重要性。但进步教育不能以此为理由将冲动和愿望视为目的，因而如果学生要参与形成激发自身发展的目的，就不能轻易地忽略细心观察、广泛的知识以及判断的需求。在一种教育的计划中，欲望和冲动的

第六章 目的的意义

发生不是最后的目的，它是形成计划和寻求方法的机会和需求。需要重申的是，这种计划只有通过研究种种情况和搜集各种相关知识，才能制订出来。

教师的任务是要确保这种可以利用的机会。因为自由的作用是进行理智的观察和判断，由此形成一种目的。教师对学生智力的练习给予指导，其目的是有助于自由，而不是限制自由。有时，教师们似乎不敢对一个团体内的成员应做什么事提出一些建议。我曾听到过这样的事，教师在学生周围堆放了一些物件和材料，听其自然，关于要用这些材料去做些什么，教师甚至不愿提供任何建议，以免侵犯了学生的自由。那么，为什么要提供这些材料呢？难道提供这些材料是某些暗示或其他什么的来源？然而，更加重要的是，在任何情况下，学生总是能够从某个地方得到有关行动的暗示。为什么一个经验更丰富和视野更广阔的人提供的建议做不到和某些出自或多或少是偶然的来源的建议一样正确？这是说不通的事情。

当然，滥用职权，强使儿童的行动遵从教师的目的而非学生的目的，这种事情也有可能发生。但是，要避免这种危险，不是让成年人完全采取退却的方式。避免这种危险的方式是：第一，教师应明智地认识到学生的能力、需要和过往的经验；第二，利用团体中各个成员所提供的进一步建议，并把它们组成整体，从而使建议发展为一种计划和设计。换句话说，这种计划是一种合作的计划，而不是一种命令。教师的建议不是用铸铁模型造出来的物体，而只是一个起点，从这个起点出发，通过学习过程中全部经验所做的贡献，把建议发展为一种计划。这种发展是通过互惠互利的给予和获得实现的。教师从学生那里获取的同时也要付出。目的的生长和形成是在社会理智的过程中实现的，这是一个根本要点。

第七章　进步主义的教材组织

　　前面已经多次提到，包含在经验中的种种客观条件及它们在未来经验的丰硕生长中所起到的促进或阻碍的作用。这就意味着，这些客观条件，不论是观察到的、记忆中的、从别人那里得来的知识，还是想象的知识，都被视为研究及学习的材料；或者，更一般地说，它们被视为学习课程的资料。然而，到目前为止，还没有明确地谈到教材问题。现在就来讨论这个话题。从经验的角度来思考教育的含义时，就很有必要考虑这件事情。凡是被称为一种学科的，不论是算术、历史、地理，还是自然科学中的一种学科，起初一定是源自日常生活经验中的材料。有些教学程序，一开始就传授经验范围以外的种种事实和真理，因而就会产生一个问题，即要找出一些方式和手段把传授的内容纳入经验的范围之内。在这方面，新教育与这些程序对比起来，有着显著的差别。毫无疑问，在早期的初等教育中，种种较新的方法取得巨大成功的一个主要原因是，它遵循的原则与旧的程序完全相反。

但是，在经验的范围之内寻找学习的材料，这仅仅是第一步。下一步是将已经经历的那些东西逐渐积累起来，发展为更充实、更丰富并且更有组织的形式，即逐渐地接近于提供给有技能的、成熟的人的那种教材形式。只要不违反教育和经验的有机联系，这种变化就是可能的。事实表明，这种变化只有在学校外面才能发生，并且与正式教育没有关系。例如，婴儿起初与种种客观事物的环境相接触，在空间和时间上都受到限制。这种环境由于经验本身固有的动力就能不断地扩大，而不需要学校教学的帮助。当婴儿学习伸手抓握、爬行、走路和说话的时候，其经验中固有的材料就扩大和加深了。当它与一些新的事物和事件发生联系时，就又产生了新的力量，而运用这些力量又能够改善和扩大其经验的内容。生命空间和时间都扩张了，环境和经验的世界就不断地生长起来，也可以说发展得越来越好。教育者接受处于婴儿期末期的孩子时，必须寻找种种方式，有意识地和慎重地对待他们前几年里依靠"本性"已经取得的成就。

上面的两种情况中，第一种情况几乎没有什么必要再予以强调。教育必须以学习者已经具有的经验作为起点，这种经验和在学习过程中发展起来的能力又为所有未来的学习提供了起点。这便是实施新教育的学校的一条主要理念。另外的一种情况，即通过经验的生长使教材的扩充和组织有序地发展，也要受到同样的关注。实际情况是否就是这样，对此我并不十分肯定。然而，教育性经验的连续性原则要求大家同样开动脑筋和予以关注去解决这方面的教育难题。毫无疑问，解决这方面的问题比起解决前一问题来更为困难。与学前儿童、幼儿园儿童和小学早期的男女儿童交往的人，很容易确定以往经验的范围或者发现与以往经验有重大关系的种种活动。对于更大一点儿的儿童，这个问题的两个方面的因素都给教育者增加了种种困难。他们越来越难发现每个人的经验背景，也很难发现如何指导经验中已经具备的材料，并把这些内容引入到更加广泛和有序的领域之中。

如果认为单纯给儿童提供某些新的经验，比起确保儿童有更熟练的技能并且更加轻松地处理自己已经熟悉的事情，更能充分地满足于把经验引导到某些不同的方面，这种观点就是错误的。把新的种种事物和事件与种种前期经验理智地联系起来，这是重要的，而且这表明，在种种事实和观念的有意识的结合方面，有了一些进展。因此，教育者的责任就在于，从现有经验的范围内，选择那些有希望、有可能提出一些新问题的事物，这些新问题能激发起新的观察和判断方式，从而扩大未来经验的范围。教师必须始终坚持把已经获得的东西当作开辟新领域的动力和手段，而非固定不变的占有物。在新的领域内，对现有的观察力和记忆力提出了新的要求。生长的连续性原则必须成为教师长久不变的座右铭。在众多行业中，教育者是最需要具备长远发展眼光之人。医生使病人恢复健康以后，就可以认为完成了自己的工作。毫无疑问，医生还有义务向病人提出有关日常生活的建议，以免将来产生同样的毛病。但是，日后的生活毕竟是病人自己的事情，而不是医生的职责，而且现时更重要的一点是，医生本人对病人未来所做的提醒和建议，说明他已经是在承担一位教育者的职能了。律师所从事的职务是替诉讼委托人把官司打赢，或者使诉讼委托人避免某些纠纷。如果律师在事情完结之后再做进一步的工作，那么他也变成一位教育者了。就教育者的工作性质而言，他负有义务去考虑自己的现时工作已经取得了什么成就，或者哪些工作还没有完成，因为未来的目标是和当前的工作紧密相连的。

这里，还需再次说明的是，进步主义教育者的问题比传统学校更为困难。传统学校的教师的确也需要向前看，但是他往往满足于仅考虑到下一个检查期或升入下一个年级的事情，除非他的性格和热情使之超越传统学校的限制。他可能在传统的学校制度所要求的范围之内去设想未来。而那些把教育与实际经验联系在一起的教师则有义务担负更加严峻和艰巨的任务。他必须通晓引导学生进入包含在已有经验中的那些新领域的可能性，并以这种知识为标准来选择和安排影响现时经验的种种情境。

传统学校的各种学科是由教材组成的，这些教材的选择和安排是根据成人的判断，认为这些内容对年轻人将来某些时候是会有用的，而这些将要学习的材料却脱离了学习者现时的生活经验。因此，这些材料只与过去有关，它只表明对过去年代的人是有用处的。本来有一种正确的观念，认为教育应当从现时经验中提取教材，应当使学生能够善于处理现时和未来的种种问题，可是人们往往把这种正确的观念误解为进步学校在极大程度上忽视过去的观念。这就走到另一个极端去了，也许这种不幸的事是自然而然产生的。如果现在和过去能够一刀两断地分割开来，那么这个结论将是正确的。但是，过去的成就提供了唯一一种可以自由运用的工具来理解现在的情况。正如个人必须回顾自己的过去才能清楚地理解他本人现在所处的情境，同样，现时社会生活中的种种问题也与过去有着密切而直接的联系，因此，学生如果不从过去探本求源，就很难理解这些问题或者找出最好的处理方式。换言之，正确的原则认为学习的目标在于未来，当前的学习材料就在现时的经验之中，这项原则能否实现取决于现时经验伸展或者说回归的程度。现时经验也能够扩展到未来，这也仅仅是因为它由于采取过去的经验而得到了扩充。

如果时间允许，讨论现在这代人未来必须加以应对的政治问题和经济问题，就可以使前面所做的一般论述更加明确和具体。除非我们知道这些问题是如何发生的，否则便不能理解其本质。引起现时社会弊病和混乱的现存机制和习俗，并非一夜之间形成的，其背后都有一段长久的历史。企图用一时一事去简单处理，其结果必定是采用肤浅的措施，最终只会使现存的问题更加严重，而且更难解决。根据脱离过去的现时知识制定的政策就好似草率粗心的个人行为。把过去当作目的的学校制度，本质上是把熟识过去当作理解当前现状的一种手段。在这个问题得到解决之前，现存的教育观念和实践之间的冲突将依然存在。一方面，将会有一些反对人士坚持主张教育的任务是传递文化遗产，他们认为这个任务即使不是唯一的，也是主要的。另一方面，也将会有一些人主张，我们不必顾及过去，而只需应对现在和未来。

到目前为止，进步学校最薄弱的一点是关于知识性教材的选择和组织，我想，这种情况是难以避免的。旧教育的主要成分是枯燥无味的教材，进步学校要从中解脱出来，是正当而合理的，同样也是不可避免的。此外，经验的领域是非常广泛的，其内容也是因时因地而变化的。对所有的进步学校来说，要求各科实行统一的课程，这是根本不可能的，这将意味着放弃了与生活经验相联系的基本原则。而且，进步学校是新的事物。进步学校的发展历程几乎不到30年。因而，在选择和组织教材时存在一定程度的不确定和含糊松散的现象，是可以预料到的。根据这一点对进步学校进行根本性的批评或抱怨，那是没有理由的。

然而，如果正在往前发展的进步教育运动未能认识到选择和组织适合于研究和学习的教材是一项根本性工作，那么大家对此做出正当的批评就是有根据的。利用各种特殊的机会，采取临时的措施，可以防止教和学固守陈规和呆板停滞。但是，基本的学习材料不能草率地信手拈来。凡是有思想自由的地方，必定会产生没有预料到的和无法预料到的机会。应该利用这些机会。但是，在活动的持续发展过程中利用这些机会和期望借此提供主要的学习材料，这两者之间存在明显的区别。

第七章 进步主义的教材组织

除非把一种特定的经验引入之前不熟悉的领域，否则，就不会发现问题。然而，只有问题才能刺激人的思考。将现时经验中发现的各种情况作为种种问题的源泉，这一特性使以经验为基础的教育与传统教育得以区分。对传统教育而言，种种问题是从经验之外产生的。然而，生长则依赖运用理智去克服现存的困难。我再重复一次，教育者的部分责任是同等对待以下两件事：第一，从现有经验的各种情况中发现问题，并且这种问题必须是在学生的能力范围之内；第二，这种问题能够激发学习者去主动地探索知识和新的观念。因此获得的一些新事实和新观念就能成为取得未来经验的基础，并且由此发现新的问题。这个过程是一个连续不断的螺旋状的过程。现在和过去不可避免的联系乃是一项并不局限于历史研究的应用原则。以自然科学为例，当代社会生活在很大程度上是应用了自然科学的结果。每个儿童和青年，不论是农村的还是城市的，其经验之所以处于现时状况，都是因为他们使用的器具利用了电、热和化学的过程。一个儿童所吃的每顿饭，无论是在准备时还是在消化时，都会涉及化学和生理学的种种原理。如果他没有接触科学所产生的作用和过程，那么他就不能利用人造灯光去阅读，也不能乘汽车和坐火车。

应该使学生通过熟悉社会上每天应用的各种物品来学习科学内容，并初步掌握各种科学事实和定律，这是一条正确的教育原则。坚持这种方法不仅是理解科学本身的最直接的途径，而且当学生更为成熟时，这也是理解现时社会里种种经济和工业问题的最有把握的途径。因为这些问题很大程度上是在商品的生产和分配中以及在服务事业中运用科学的产物,而服务事业乃是决定人类和社会团体彼此之间现时关系的最重要的因素。有一种主张认为,类似于实验室和研究机构中的研究过程不是儿童日常生活经验的一部分,因而,它们不属于以经验为基础的教育范畴。这种观点是荒谬的。未成年人不能采用成熟的专家的研究方法去研究科学的种种事实和原理,这是不言而喻的。但是,这个事实给教师提出了一个重要的问题。这个事实并不能使教师免除利用现时的种种经验的责任,以便通过掌握种种事实和定律,可以逐渐地引导学习者体验科学规则。

如果现存的经验,在细节和广义上都确实是由应用科学引起的,那么,首先要把科学应用到产品的生产和分配过程以及服务事业上面,其次,要把科学应用到人类维持社交的种种关系上面。如此说来,教育必须引导学习者在构成科学的最后组织中取得完全相同的事实和原理,否则,学习者就不可能理解当前的各种社会势力(不理解社会势力就不能掌握和控制它们)。让学习者熟悉科学的教材,这条原则的重要性停留在对现时社会问题的见解之上。科学的种种方法也能提示建立较好的社会秩序所要采用的种种策略和政策。现存的种种社会条件很大程度上源自科学的应用,但是在可能的范围内,科学还没有得到充分的应用。因为到目前为止,科学的应用或多或少地具有偶然性并且受到目的的影响,例如私人利益和私人权力之类的目的,这些大都是在近代科学发展以前的时代中各种制度传承下来的产物。

第七章 进步主义的教材组织

我们几乎每天都从各种渠道听到一种说法，即人类不可能理智地指导他们的共同生活。一方面，我们听说人类关系（即国内的和国际的种种关系）的复杂性，另一方面，人类大都是些具有感情和习惯的动物，这个事实使得人类不可能运用理智进行大规模的社会计划和管理。如果从儿童的早期教育开始，并通过持续不断的研究和学习，做出各种系统化的努力，期望把经过科学验证的理智的方法作为最主要的教育方法，那么，这种观点将是更为可信的。在习惯的固有本性中，没有任何东西能够阻止理智的方法变得习以为常；同时，在情绪的本性中也没有任何东西可以阻止对理智的方法产生强烈的专一情绪。

这里采用的科学实例是为了说明可以在现时的经验中对教材做出不断进步的选择，其目的是形成一种组织：这种组织是自由的，而非从外部强加的，因为其遵照经验本身的生长规律。利用学习者的现时生活经验中的教材以达到学习科学的目的，这也许是一种基本原则的最好例证。这种原则就是，相对于教育性生长中所得的经验而言，用现有经验作为一种工具，将学习者带入一个更广阔、更精致、更有序的周围世界，包括物质的世界和人类的世界。霍格本（Hogben）的新近著作《大众数学》（*Mathematics for the Million*）表明，如果把数学看作文明的镜子和文明进步的主要动力，那么数学确实能像各种自然科学一样，对于达成预期目标做出贡献。无论如何，对不断进步的知识进行组织一直是根本的理想。关于知识的组织，我们很有可能发现种种非此即彼的哲学，它们是最为活跃的。实际上，如果说得简单一点儿，即人们时常认为，传统教育从知识的组织概念出发，几乎完全忽视现时的生活经验，既然如此，那么以生活经验为基础的教育应当也是轻视那种关于种种事实和观念的组织的。

刚才，我曾把这种组织叫作一种理想，我的意思是指，从消极方面来说，教育者不能以已经组织好的知识为起点，并把这些知识按照一定的分量配成若干份，一勺一勺地倒给学生。但是，作为一种理想，有关事实和观念的主动组织过程永远是一种现时的教育过程。如果不是为了让人们了解更多的事实，产生更多的想法，并将两者更加优化有序地进行安排，那么这种经验是没有教育意义的。有一种观点认为组织是一种与经验无关的原则，那是不正确的。否则，经验就将变得分散乃至混乱。少年儿童的经验集中于一些人和家庭之中。现在精神病学者已经认识到，家庭中的正常秩序遭到破坏，乃是日后精神上和情绪上种种弊病的最深重的根源——这一事实也证实了这种组织的真实性。在早期学校教育中，在幼儿园和低年级中，一种巨大的进展是维护了社会与人在经验组织中的核心地位，而不像早先的旧教育那样激烈地改变这个重心。但是教育中的一个突出的问题，与音乐中的突出问题一样，是转调。就教育而言，所谓转调是指把以社会和人为中心的活动转向更客观的、更理智的组织计划。然而，要经常记住，理智的组织本身不是目的，而是一种手段，用这种手段可以理解和更为明智地安排种种社会关系，特别是安排人与人之间的关系和纽带。

第七章 进步主义的教材组织

当教育在理论和实践上都是以经验作为基础时,由成年人和专家编制的教材不能当作起点,这是毋庸置疑的。然而,这类教材代表了教育应当不断前进的目标。知识的科学编制最基本的原则之一是因果原则,这几乎是无须说明的。科学家理解和说明这一条原则的方法,与儿童经验中获取这一原则的方法当然有所不同。但是,无论是这种因果关系,还是对这种关系的理解,都与儿童的经验存在一定的联系。当一个两三岁的孩子懂得不可以太靠近火焰,而且知道靠近火炉的适当地方就可以取暖时,他就理解了并且在运用这种因果关系。任何理智的活动都符合这种因果关系的要求,而且理智的程度取决于其不仅符合而且将此原则铭记于心间的程度。

在较早期经验的形式中,因果关系本身不是以抽象的形式呈现,而是表现为手段和目的两者之间的关系,表现为种种方法和种种结果之间的关系。判断力和理解力的成长,在本质上就是发展形成目的并为实现这一目的而选择和安排方法的能力。儿童的最初经验中充满了方法和结果关系的各种实例,做一餐饭和一种照明的光源都能用来证明这种关系。教育上的困难不在于缺乏以方法和结果的关系来证明因果关系的种种情境,而在于无法利用其来引导学习者去理解特定经验实例中的这种关系,这种现象极为普遍。逻辑学家所说的"分析与综合",就是选择和组织实现某种目的的方法。

这一原则为在学校中利用种种活动奠定了首要的基础。在教育工作中,企求学校中主动性作业的多样化,而同时又谴责不断更新知识和观念组织的必要性，没有比这种主张更为荒唐的了。理智的活动和无目的的活动是有区别的。理智的活动是从多种多样的现时情况中选择出方法来——这便是分析；它还要安排这些被选择出来的方法达到预期的目标或目的——这便是综合。显然，学习者越不成熟，其所预期的目的必定越简单，所使用的方法也越低级。但是，以理解某些结果与方法之间的关系为根据的活动的组织原则，即使对年龄很小的儿童也是适用的。相反，如果一种活动是盲目的，那么这种活动就没有教育作用了。随着成熟程度的增加，各种方法的相互关系问题变得更为急迫。理智的观察从方法与目的的关系转变到更为复杂的各种方法彼此之间的相互关系问题，随着转变程度的提高，原因和结果的观念变得更加显著和明确。认为学校中应当有商店、厨房等的最终理由并不只是因为这些场所提供活动的机会，而是在于它们为这类活动提供机会，或者为获得手工技能提供机会，引导学生注意方法和目的之间的关系，并且引导其考虑事物之间相互作用会产生特定结果的方式。在原则上，它与科学研究应有实验室的理由是相同的。

除非知识的组织问题能够依据经验得以解决，否则一定会产生反作用，趋向于外部强加的组织方法。这种反作用已经有了明显的迹象。我们曾听说，无论是老学校还是新学校，在完成主要任务方面都失败了。据说，学校没有发展学生批判性的辨别能力和推理能力。我们曾听说，由于学生积累了各种各样难以消化的知识，由于学生企图获得在商业界立竿见影的各种形式的技能，其思考能力被窒息。我们曾听说，这些弊端来自科学的影响，来自夸大了的各种现时需要，从而牺牲了历史传承下来的历经考验的文化遗产。有人坚持说，必须把科学及其方法放在次要的地位；我们必须回到亚里士多德和圣·托马斯逻辑学体系中所提出的第一原理的根本逻辑，以使年轻人在他们的理智和道德生活中找到确实可靠的停泊点，不致随风摆动。

假如在学校的所有学科的日常工作中，一以贯之地采用科学的方法，那么这种情绪上的诉求会给我留下更深的印象。实际上，我认为要使教育工作不致漫无目标地随波逐流，必须在两种办法中选择出一种。一种办法是企图引导教育者回到科学方法还没有建立以前的几个世纪就早已出现的种种理智的方法和观念上面。这种办法在情绪上、理智上以及经济上总体不太稳定的时期里，也许能够暂时获得成功。因为在这些情况下，人们依赖固定权威的欲望是非常强烈的。然而，这种办法完全远离现代生活的情形，让我认为想从这条道路上寻求解救是愚蠢的。另一种可供选择的办法是系统地利用科学的方法，以此作为模式和理想来对经验内部固有的可能性进行理智探索和开发。

这个问题所涉及的各个方面对进步学校具有特殊的影响。如果无法持续关注种种经验的理智内容的发展，无法获得日益增长的种种事实和观念的组织，那么最终只会增强一种反作用力，回到理智和道德的权威主义。现时经验并不是获取科学方法的时机和场合。

但是科学方法的某些特点,与任何以经验为基础的教育计划都有着紧密的联系,必须得以关注。

第一,相比其他方法,科学的实验方法对观念给予更多的重视,而不是更少。如果行动不受某些主要的观念指导,那就没有所谓的科学意义上的实验。观念被用来作为假设,而不是最后的真理,为什么观念在科学中比其他任何地方都要受到细心的查看和检验,原因就在于此。当观念本身被视为头等真理时,就没有任何理由再做小心翼翼的考察了。人们接受其作为不变的真理,事情就此完结了。但是,作为假设,它们就必须不断地被检验和修正,被要求精确地阐述。

第二,依据观念或假设所进行的活动产生出一些结果来,由这些结果来验证观念或假设。这个事实表明,必须细心地有区别地观察活动的结果。一种活动所引起的结果如果没有受到观察的检验,也许暂时会让人感到高兴。但是,它在理智上没有任何成效。这种活动不能提供关于产生活动的种种情境的知识,也不能澄清和扩展观念。

第三,在实验方法中所表现出的理智的方法要求人们记住种种观念、活动和观察到的结果。所谓记住就是反省回顾和总结,对经验发展中的重要特点既要分辨清楚,又要记录下来。反省就是回顾过去做过的事项,以便从中提取最终的含义,这些含义对于明智地处理未来的经验是一种主要的资源。这便是理智组织和心智训练的核心。

我必须用一般的语言，而且经常是抽象的语言来表述自己的思想。但是，前述内容和下述的一种要求是有机地联系在一起的。这种要求是，为了使经验具有教育作用，必须将其引入正在扩展的教材领域之中，即延伸到关于事实或知识以及观念的教学内容中去。只有教育者把教和学视为不断继续的经验改造，才能达到这种要求。只有当教育者具备长远的眼光，把每一个现时的经验视为影响未来经验本质的一种动力，才能依次达到上述要求。我意识到，自己对科学方法的重视可能会有些误导性，因为它可能让人只是想到专家在实验室里所使用的专门技术。但是，我所强调的科学方法的意义与专门技术毫无关系。科学的方法意指了解日常生活经验意义的唯一可靠且可控的方法。它的意思是，科学的方法提供一种工作模式和各种条件使得经验继续向前、向外扩展。教育者所面临的问题是：使方法适应于具有不同成熟程度的各种人。在这个问题中一些不变的因素是：观念的形成、依据观念的行动、对各种情况的观察以及为了将来的使用而对种种事实和观念加以组织。不论是种种观念、活动，还是观察、组织，对一个6岁的儿童与对一个12岁或18岁的青少年来说，都是不同的，更不必说与成年的科学家相比了。但是，如果经验实际上是有教育作用的，那么在每一个阶段里经验都会有所扩展。因而，不论在经验发展的哪一个阶段，我们要么按照经验提供的模式去做，要么采取另一种办法，即在发展和控制活生生的动态经验时忽略理智的作用，除此之外，别无他途。

第八章　经验——教育的方法和目标

在我上面的讨论中，我曾经假定原则的合理性，即为了实现教育目的，不论对学习者个人来说，还是对社会来说，教育必须根植于经验——这种经验常常是一些个人实际的生活经验。我并不赞成这个原则，也不企图证实这个原则。教育上的保守主义者和激进主义者，对于当前教育的整个状况，都是深为不满的。在代表这两派教育思想的有识之士之间，至少在这方面有许多一致之处：教育制度必须朝着这条路或另一条路前进，即或者是倒退到前科学时代的理智和道德标准之中，或者尽量利用科学方法，以便发展扩大经验生长的种种可能性。我只是尽力指出一些条件，如果教育沿着后一条路前进，就必须令人满意地实现这些条件。

我是如此相信教育的潜力，以至当教育被看作对日常经验中固有的种种可能性的发展给予理智的指导时，我认为不需要在这里批评另一条路线，也不必发起争论以支持采取经验的路线。采取这种中间道路可以预料到的唯一可导致失败的原因，我认为是经验和实验的方法尚难以满足需要。在世界上没有一种训练像经验的训练那样严格地受到理智的发展和指导的检验，因此，新教育的标准、目标和方法暂时受到了人们的反对，我所能了解到的唯一理由是：一些教育者表面上自称采纳了新教育的标准、目标和方法，但是实际上在实践中难以为继。我曾多次强调过，新教育的道路并不比老路容易走，而是一条更艰辛和更困难的道路。除非新教育得到大多数人的支持，否则，其处境将会依然如故。而要使大多数人都支持，那就需要信奉新教育的人为此严肃认真、齐心协力地持续工作。我相信，新教育未来的最大危险在于大家都认为它是一条容易走的路，以至于新教育的进程成为毫无准备的临时举动，即使不是这样，那至少也几乎是过一天算一天，过一周算一周。出于这个原因，我并不颂扬新教育的种种原则，而仅仅是说明某些必须具备的条件。有了这些条件，新教育会在成功的路途上飞奔前进，这是理所当然的。

先前我经常使用"进步"教育和"新"教育这些名称。然而，在本文结束时，我仍要表明我的坚定的信念。我坚信，根本的问题并不在于新教育和旧教育的对比，也不在于进步教育和传统教育的对比，而在于究竟什么东西才有资格配得上"教育"这一术语。我希望且相信，我并不仅仅是因为任何目的和方法而采用了"进步主义"的名称，就去赞成这些目的和方法。根本的问题在于教育本身的性质，而不在于给它加上什么修饰的形容词。我们所需要的教育，是纯粹和简单的教育。当我们专心致力于寻求教育究竟是什么，以及具备什么条件才能实现这种教育，而不是使它停留在术语或口号上时，我们就能取得更实际、更迅速的进步。我强调一种合理的经验哲学的必要性,这是唯一的理由。

杜威生平与主要著作年表[1]

1859年

10月20日约翰·杜威（John Dewey）出生于美国佛蒙特州伯灵顿市的一个村庄。

1875年

中学毕业。

1875—1879年

在佛蒙特大学读书。

1879年

获文学学士学位。成为美国大学生联谊会成员。

1879—1881年

任宾夕法尼亚州石油城中学教师，讲授拉丁文、代数和自然学科等课程。

---

[1] 摘编自：杜威，等. 杜威传 [M]. 修订版. 单中惠，编译. 合肥：安徽教育出版社，2009：435—440；杜威. 我们怎样思维·经验与教育 [M]. 姜文闵，译. 北京：人民教育出版社，2015：299—303.——译者注

1881—1882年

任佛蒙特州夏洛特村莱克维尤高级中学教师。跟佛蒙特大学的托里（H. A. P. Torrey）教授学习哲学史。

1882—1884年

在约翰斯·霍普金斯大学攻读博士学位。1883年春讲授本科生哲学史课程。

1884年

获得哲学博士学位，博士学位论文是《康德的心理学》（未公开发表）。

1884—1888年

任密歇根大学哲学系讲师和助理教授。

1885年

发表第一篇教育论文《教育与妇女健康》（Education and the Health of Women）（载《科学》杂志1885年10月16日）。

1886年

7月与艾丽斯·奇普曼（Alice Chipman）结婚。出版第一本心理学著作《心理学》（*Psychology*）。

1888—1889年

任明尼苏达大学哲学教授。

1889—1894年

任密歇根大学哲学系教授和系主任。

1893年

发表第一篇关于中等教育的论文《中学的伦理学教学》(Teaching

Ethics in the High School）（载《教育评论》杂志11月号）。

1894—1904年

任芝加哥大学哲学、心理学和教育学系主任。讲授研究生课程。

1896—1903年

领导芝加哥大学实验学校。在《一个教育学实验》（A Pedagogical Experiment）（载《幼儿园杂志》1896年6月号）和《大学学校》(The University School)（载《芝加哥大学学报》1896年11月4日）等文章中，杜威对"芝加哥大学实验学校"（杜威学校）的实验做了论述。

1896年

发表《与意志训练有关的兴趣》（Interest in Relation to Training of Will）。

1897年

发表《我的教育信条》（My Pedagogic Creed）、《教育中的伦理原则》（Ethical Principles Underlying Education）。

1899年

出版《学校与社会》(The School and Society)（1915年出版修订本）。

1899—1900年

任美国心理学联合会会长。

1902年

发表《儿童与课程》（The Child and the Curriculum）、《教育的情境》（The Educational Situation）。

1902—1904年

任芝加哥大学教育学院院长。

1904年

被授予威斯康星大学名誉法学博士学位。

1904—1930年

任哥伦比亚大学哲学教授。

1905—1906年

任美国哲学学会会长。

1908年

出版《伦理学》（*Ethics*）[与詹姆斯·H. 塔夫茨（James H. Tufts）合著，1932年出版修订本]。

1909年

出版《教育中的道德原理》（*Moral Principles in Education*）。

1910年

出版《我们怎样思维》（*How We Think*）（1933年出版修订本）、《达尔文对哲学的影响》（*The Influence of Darwin on Philosophy*）。被授予佛蒙特大学名誉法学博士学位。

1913年

出版《教育中的兴趣和努力》（*Interest and Effort in Education*）。被授予密歇根大学名誉法学博士学位。

1915年

出版《明日之学校》（*Schools of Tomorrow*）[与女儿伊夫琳·杜威（Evelyn Dewey）合著]。创立美国大学教授联合会并任第一任会长。被授予约翰斯·霍普金斯大学名誉法学博士学位。

1916年

出版《民主主义与教育》（*Democracy and Education*）、《实验逻辑论文集》（*Essays in Experimental Logic*）。

1917年

被授予伊利诺伊学院名誉法学博士学位。

1919—1921年

在北京大学和南京高等师范学校等学校演讲。

1920年

出版《来自中国和日本的通信》（*Letters from China and Japan*）（与妻子艾丽斯·奇普曼合著）。被授予北京大学名誉法学博士学位。

1922年

出版《人性与行为》（*Human Nature and Conduct*）。

1924年

在土耳其研究教育状况。

1925年

出版《经验与自然》（*Experience and Nature*）（1929年出版修订本）。

1926年

在墨西哥研究教育状况。

1927年

妻子艾丽斯·奇普曼去世。

1928年

在苏联研究教育状况。任美国进步教育协会名誉会长。发表《进步教育与教育科学》(Progressive Education and the Science of Education)。

1929年

出版《人物与事件》(Characters and Events)。发表《确定性的寻求》(The Quest for Certainty)、《教育科学的资源》(The Sources of a Science of Education)。被授予哥伦比亚大学名誉法学博士学位。

1930年

发表《旧个人主义与新个人主义》(Individualism Old and New)。被授予法国巴黎大学名誉法学博士学位。

1930—1939年

任哥伦比亚大学荣誉退休教授。

1931年

发表《哲学与文明》(Philosophy and Civilization)、《从教育混乱中寻找出路》(The Way Out of Educational Confusion)。

1932年

被授予哈佛大学名誉法学博士学位。

1934年

出版《艺术即经验》(Art as Experience)、《一种普通的信仰》(A Common Faith)。

1935年

出版《自由与社会行动》(*Freedom and Social Action*)。

1938年

出版《经验与教育》(*Experience and Education*)、《逻辑：探究的理论》(*Logic: The Theory of Inquiry*)。

1939年

出版《自由与文化》(*Freedom and Culture*)、《价值的学说》(*Theory of Valuation*)。

1941年

出版《伯特兰·罗素案件》(*The Bertrand Russell Case*)[与霍勒斯·M. 卡伦（Horace M. Kallen）合编]。

1946年

出版《人的问题》(*Problems of Men*)。12月与罗伯塔·L. 格兰特（Roberta L. Grant）结婚。被授予挪威奥斯陆大学荣誉哲学博士学位、宾夕法尼亚大学名誉理学博士学位。

1949年

出版《认知与所知》(*Knowing and the Known*)[与阿瑟·F. 本特利（Arthur F. Bentley）合著]。

1952年

发表最后一篇教育论文《〈教育资源的使用〉一书的引言》(*Introduction to the Use of Resources in Education*)。

1952年

6月1日在纽约去世。

译 后 记

展现在读者面前的这本小册子,是约翰·杜威(John Dewey,1859—1952)在1938年出版的一部著作。杜威著述等身,对学校教育的革新身体力行,对教育理论的发展贡献非凡,是伟大的哲学家、心理学家、教育理论家和学校改革实践家。

1991年,乔·安·博伊兹顿(Jon Ann Boydston)博士曾主编出版了37卷本的《杜威著作全集》(*The Collected Works of John Dewey*,1882—1953)。我们不妨简单地列出杜威重要的教育著作出版年份:《我的教育信条》(1897年),《学校与社会》(1899年),《儿童与课程》(1902年),《伦理学:道德生活的理论》(1906年),《我们怎样思维》(1910年),《明日之学校》(1915年),《民主主义与教育》(1916年),《经验与教育》(1938年),《自由与文化》(1939年)。从这里我们可以看出,《经验与教育》是杜威在对自己40年来的教育思想与改革实践进行反思的基础上写成的。

曾有人评论道:"《经验与教育》代表了20世纪最重要的教育理论家最精练的教育思想。此外,它也许是杜威作品中最简明扼要、最通俗易懂且意义最深刻的一部。"我基本上同意这一评论。我认为,本书确实是反映杜威教育思想的最重要的著作之一,是杜威对几十年新旧教育论争和实践发展的反思,确实是杜威著作中简明扼要和意义深刻的代表作,也确实不算是深奥难懂。要言不烦,杜威在本书中指出了如何在经验与教育两者之间建立起一种和谐共生的关系。

生活、社会、教育、学校、儿童、发展、经验、民主、进步……这些都是杜威教育思想中最重要的词汇,影响了几代人,并将一直发挥启迪作用。杜威最著名的教育思想可以说是大家都熟悉的一句名言:"教育即生活,学校即社会"。这是杜威留给后人的教育思想遗产之精髓。在本书中,杜威主要阐述了经验与教育之间的关系。教育离不开经验,但并不是所有的经验都有教育价值。问题是要分析什么样的经验,在什么时候,在什么场景下,对什么样的人具有教育价值。也许我们可以这样说:教育就是要依托经验、运用经验和改造经验。依托就是指以经验为前提;没有经验,就没有教育。运用经验就是指在教育中一定要运用从主体自身提取的经验、从同伴那里借鉴的经验和从外部来源那里刚学会的经验。受教育的过程就是运用经验的过程。无经验当然是无教育,但是有了经验就一定要及时运用,否则就等于浪费了经验。把经验运用在什么地方、什么时机,以及运用多少数量的经验,这是具体辩证的事情。改造经验是目的本身,经验得以改造之后,就是经验发展了、丰富了、深入了、个性化了和有独特性了。依托经验是为了运用经验,运用经验是为了改造经验,改造后的经验又成为新的依托经验,这样学习和教育

译后记

就得以循环、延续和发展。

我们一直把杜威看成进步主义的旗手,认为他倡导以儿童为中心,反对"传统教育"那一套腐朽的东西。但是在本书中,杜威强调"传统教育"和"进步教育"都有各自的缺陷,两者都没有应用完备的经验哲学,都可能产生错误的教育导向。杜威在本书中花了大量篇幅来说明他的经验哲学及其与教育的关系。杜威敦促所有旨在寻找教育领域新方向的教师和教育工作者考虑层次更深、范围更广的教育问题,不要陷入各种"主义之争",要尊重出自各种来源的经验,给学生提供一种既是历史的又是社会的、既是有序的又是动态的真实学习情境。

在当今这样一个变化加剧的社会中,我们重温杜威的《经验与教育》尤感必要。我们了解历史是为了更好地适应现在和创造未来。让我们大家一起来读一读《经验与教育》。我为自己有机会参与翻译这本小册子而感到高兴。我衷心感谢"万千教育"的石铁先生和吴红先生,他们向经典致敬的教育情怀影响了我。我在翻译中参考了其他专家翻译出版的译本,博士生方向和钟丽佳协助我完成了翻译工作,在此一并表示衷心的感谢。当然,我也深知,我对这本书的翻译未必非常胜任并令人满意,欢迎读者对我翻译中出现的不妥之处提出批评意见。

盛群力

(浙江大学教育学院教授,博士生导师)

2016年3月20日于杭州

Experience and Education

经验与教育

（英文版）

John Dewey

PREFACE

All social movements involve conflicts which are reflected intellectually in controversies. It would not be a sign of health if such an important social interest as education were not also an arena of struggles, practical and theoretical. But for theory, at least for the theory that forms a philosophy of education, the practical conflicts and the controversies that are conducted upon the level of these conflicts, only set a problem. It is the business of an intelligent theory of education to ascertain the causes for the conflicts that exist and then, instead of taking one side or the other, to indicate a plan of operations proceeding from a level deeper and more inclusive than is represented by the practices and ideas of the contending parties.

This formulation of the business of the philosophy of education does not mean that the latter should attempt to bring about a compromise between opposed schools of thought, to find a *via media*, nor yet make an eclectic combination of points picked out hither and yon from all schools. It means the necessity of the introduction of a new order of conceptions leading to new modes of practice. It is for this reason that it is so difficult to develop a philosophy of education, the moment tradition and custom are departed from. It is for this reason that the conduct of schools, based upon a new order of conceptions, is so much more difficult than is the management of schools which walk in beaten paths. Hence, every movement in the direction of a new order of ideas and of activities directed by them calls out, sooner or later, a return to what appear to be simpler and more fundamental ideas and practices of the past — as is exemplified at present in education in the attempt to revive the principles of ancient Greece and of the middle ages.

It is in this context that I have suggested at the close of this little volume that those who are looking ahead to a new movement in education, adapted to the existing need for a new social order, should think in terms of Education itself rather than in terms of some 'ism about education, even such an 'ism as "progressivism." For in spite of itself any movement that thinks and acts in terms of an 'ism becomes so involved in reaction against other 'isms that it is unwittingly controlled by them. For it then forms its principles by reaction against them instead of by a comprehensive, constructive survey of actual needs, problems, and possibilities. Whatever value is possessed by the essay presented in this little volume resides in its attempt to call attention to the larger and deeper issues of Education so as to suggest their proper frame of reference.

John Dewey

CHAPTER 1

TRADITIONAL VS. PROGRESSIVE EDUCATION

Mankind likes to think in terms of extreme opposites. It is given to formulating its beliefs in terms of *Either-Ors*, between which it recognizes no intermediate possibilities. When forced to recognize that the extremes cannot be acted upon, it is still inclined to hold that they are all right in theory but that when it comes to practical matters circumstances compel us to compromise. Educational philosophy is no exception. The history of educational theory is marked by opposition between the idea that education is development from within and that it is formation from without; that it is based upon natural endowments and that education is a process of overcoming natural inclination and substituting in its place habits acquired under external pressure.

At present, the opposition, so far as practical affairs of the school are concerned, tends to take the form of contrast between traditional and progressive education. If the underlying ideas of the former are formulated broadly, without the qualifications required for accurate statement, they are found to be about as follows: The subject-matter of education consists of bodies of information and of skills that have been worked out in the past; therefore, the chief business of the school is to transmit them to the new generation. In the past, there have also been developed standards and rules of conduct; moral training consists in forming habits of action in conformity with these rules and standards. Finally, the general pattern of school organization (by which I mean the relations of pupils to one another and to the teachers) constitutes the school a kind of institution sharply marked off from other social institutions. Call up in imagination the ordinary schoolroom, its time-schedules, schemes of classification, of examination and promotion, of rules of order, and I think you will grasp what is meant by "pattern of organization." If then you contrast this scene with what goes on in the family, for example, you will appreciate what is meant by the school being a kind of institution sharply marked off from any other form of social organization.

The three characteristics just mentioned fix the aims and methods of instruction and discipline. The main purpose or objective is to prepare the young for future responsibilities and for success in life, by means of acquisition of the organized bodies of information and

Chapter 1 Traditional vs. Progressive Education

prepared forms of skill which comprehend the material of instruction. Since the subject-matter as well as standards of proper conduct are handed down from the past, the attitude of pupils must, upon the whole, be one of docility, receptivity, and obedience. Books, especially textbooks, are the chief representatives of the lore and wisdom of the past, while teachers are the organs through which pupils are brought into effective connection with the material. Teachers are the agents through which knowledge and skills are communicated and rules of conduct enforced.

I have not made this brief summary for the purpose of criticizing the underlying philosophy. The rise of what is called new education and progressive schools is of itself a product of discontent with traditional education. In effect it is a criticism of the latter. When the implied criticism is made explicit it reads somewhat as follows: The traditional scheme is, in essence, one of imposition from above and from outside. It imposes adult standards, subject-matter, and methods upon those who are only growing slowly toward maturity. The gap is so great that the required subject-matter, the methods of learning and of behaving are foreign to the existing capacities of the young. They are beyond the reach of the experience the young learners already possess. Consequently, they must be imposed; even though good teachers will use devices of art to cover up the imposition so as to relieve it of obviously brutal features.

But the gulf between the mature or adult products and the experience and abilities of the young is so wide that the very situation forbids much active participation by pupils in the development of what is taught. Theirs is to do — and learn, as it was the part of the six hundred to do and die. Learning here means acquisition of what already is incorporated in books and in the heads of the elders. Moreover, that which is taught is thought of as essentially static. It is taught as a finished product, with little regard either to the ways in which it was originally built up or to changes that will surely occur in the future. It is to a large extent the cultural product of societies that assumed the future would be much like the past, and yet it is used as educational food in a society where change is the rule, not the exception.

If one attempts to formulate the philosophy of education implicit in the practices of the new education, we may, I think, discover certain common principles amid the variety of progressive schools now existing. To imposition from above is opposed expression and cultivation of individuality; to external discipline is opposed free activity; to learning from texts and teachers, learning through experience; to acquisition of isolated skills and techniques by drill, is opposed acquisition of them as means of attaining ends which make direct vital appeal; to preparation for a more or less remote future is opposed making the most of the opportunities of present life; to static

Chapter 1 Traditional vs. Progressive Education

aims and materials is opposed acquaintance with a changing world.

Now, all principles by themselves are abstract. They become concrete only in the consequences which result from their application. Just because the principles set forth are so fundamental and far-reaching, everything depends upon the interpretation given them as they are put into practice in the school and the home. It is at this point that the reference made earlier to *Either-Or* philosophies becomes peculiarly pertinent. The general philosophy of the new education may be sound, and yet the difference in abstract principles will not decide the way in which the moral and intellectual preference involved shall be worked out in practice. There is always the danger in a new movement that in rejecting the aims and methods of that which it would supplant, it may develop its principles negatively rather than positively and constructively. Then it takes its clew in practice from that which is rejected instead of from the constructive development of its own philosophy.

I take it that the fundamental unity of the newer philosophy is found in the idea that there is an intimate and necessary relation between the processes of actual experience and education. If this be true, then a positive and constructive development of its own basic idea depends upon having a correct idea of experience. Take, for example, the question of organized subject-matter—which will be discussed in some detail later. The problem for progressive education is: What is the place and meaning of subject-matter and of organization *within* experience? How does subject-matter function? Is there anything inherent in experience which tends towards progressive organization of its contents? What results follow when the materials of experience are not progressively organized? A philosophy which proceeds on the basis of rejection, of sheer opposition, will neglect these questions. It will tend to suppose that because the old education was based on ready-made organization, therefore it suffices to reject the principle of organization *in toto*, instead of striving to discover what it means and how it is to be attained on the basis of experience. We might go through all the points of difference between the new and the old education and reach similar conclusions. When external control is rejected, the problem becomes that of finding the factors of control that are inherent within experience. When external authority is rejected, it does not follow that all authority should be rejected, but rather that there is need to search for a more effective source of authority. Because the older education imposed the knowledge, methods, and the rules of conduct of the mature person upon the young, it does not follow, except upon the basis of the extreme *Either-Or* philosophy, that the knowledge and skill of the mature person has no directive value for the experience of the immature. On the contrary, basing education upon personal experience may mean more multiplied and more intimate contacts between the mature

Chapter 1 Traditional vs. Progressive Education

and the immature than ever existed in the traditional school, and consequently more, rather than less, guidance by others. The problem, then, is: how these contacts can be established without violating the principle of learning through personal experience. The solution of this problem requires a well thought-out philosophy of the social factors that operate in the constitution of individual experience.

What is indicated in the foregoing remarks is that the general principles of the new education do not of themselves solve any of the problems of the actual or practical conduct and management of progressive schools. Rather, they set new problems which have to be worked out on the basis of a new philosophy of experience. The problems are not even recognized, to say nothing of being solved, when it is assumed that it suffices to reject the ideas and practices of the old education and then go to the opposite extreme. Yet I am sure that you will appreciate what is meant when I say that many of the newer schools tend to make little or nothing of organized subject-matter of study; to proceed as if any form of direction and guidance by adults were an invasion of individual freedom, and as if the idea that education should be concerned with the present and future meant that acquaintance with the past has little or no role to play in education. Without pressing these defects to the point of exaggeration, they at least illustrate what is meant by a theory and practice of education which proceeds negatively or by reaction against what has been current in education rather than by a positive and constructive development of purposes, methods, and subject-matter on the foundation of a theory of experience and its educational potentialities.

It is not too much to say that an educational philosophy which professes to be based on the idea of freedom may become as dogmatic as ever was the traditional education which is reacted against. For any theory and set of practices is dogmatic which is not based upon critical examination of its own underlying principles. Let us say that the new education emphasizes the freedom of the learner. Very well. A problem is now set. What does freedom mean and what are the conditions under which it is capable of realization? Let us say that the kind of external imposition which was so common in the traditional school limited rather than promoted the intellectual and moral development of the young. Again, very well. Recognition of this serious defect sets a problem. Just what is the role of the teacher and of books in promoting the educational development of the immature? Admit that traditional education employed as the subject-matter for study facts and ideas so bound up with the past as to give little help in dealing with the issues of the present and future. Very well. Now we have the problem of discovering the connection which actually exists *within* experience between the achievements of the past and the issues of the present. We have the problem of ascertaining how acquaintance with the past may be translated into a potent

Chapter 1　Traditional vs. Progressive Education

instrumentality for dealing effectively with the future. We may reject knowledge of the past as the *end* of education and thereby only emphasize its importance as a *means*. When we do that we have a problem that is new in the story of education: How shall the young become acquainted with the past in such a way that the acquaintance is a potent agent in appreciation of the living present?

CHAPTER 2

THE NEED OF A THEORY OF EXPERIENCE

In short, the point I am making is that rejection of the philosophy and practice of traditional education sets a new type of difficult educational problem for those who believe in the new type of education. We shall operate blindly and in confusion until we recognize this fact; until we thoroughly appreciate that departure from the old solves no problems. What is said in the following pages is, accordingly, intended to indicate some of the main problems with which the newer education is confronted and to suggest the main lines along which their solution is to be sought. I assume that amid all uncertainties there is one permanent frame of reference: namely, the organic connection between education and personal experience; or, that the new philosophy of education is committed to some kind of empirical and experimental philosophy. But experience and experiment are not self-explanatory ideas. Rather, their meaning is part of the problem to be explored. To know the meaning of empiricism we need to understand what experience is.

The belief that all genuine education comes about through experience does not mean that all experiences are genuinely or equally educative. Experience and education cannot be directly equated to each other. For some experiences are mis-educative. Any experience is mis-educative that has the effect of arresting or distorting the growth of further experience. An experience may be such as to engender callousness; it may produce lack of sensitivity and of responsiveness. Then the possibilities of having richer experience in the future are restricted. Again, a given experience may increase a person's automatic skill in a particular direction and yet tend to land him in a groove or rut; the effect again is to narrow the field of further experience. An experience may be immediately enjoyable and yet promote the formation of a slack and careless attitude; this attitude then operates to modify the quality of subsequent experiences so as to prevent a person from getting out of them what they have to give. Again, experiences may be so disconnected from one another that, while each is agreeable or even exciting in itself, they are not linked cumulatively to one another. Energy is then dissipated and a person becomes scatterbrained. Each experience may be lively, vivid, and "interesting," and yet their disconnectedness may artificially generate dispersive, disintegrated, centrifugal habits. The consequence of

Chapter 2 The Need of a Theory of Experience

formation of such habits is inability to control future experiences. They are then taken, either by way of enjoyment or of discontent and revolt, just as they come. Under such circumstances, it is idle to talk of self-control.

Traditional education offers a plethora of examples of experiences of the kinds just mentioned. It is a great mistake to suppose, even tacitly, that the traditional schoolroom was not a place in which pupils had experiences. Yet this is tacitly assumed when progressive education as a plan of learning by experience is placed in sharp opposition to the old. The proper line of attack is that the experiences which were had, by pupils and teachers alike, were largely of a wrong kind. How many students, for example, were rendered callous to ideas, and how many lost the impetus to learn because of the way in which learning was experienced by them? How many acquired special skills by means of automatic drill so that their power of judgment and capacity to act intelligently in new situations was limited? How many came to associate the learning process with ennui and boredom? How many found what they did learn so foreign to the situations of life outside the school as to give them no power of control over the latter? How many came to associate books with dull drudgery, so that they were "conditioned" to all but flashy reading matter?

If I ask these questions, it is not for the sake of wholesale condemnation of the old education. It is for quite another purpose. It is to emphasize the fact, first, that young people in traditional schools do have experiences; and, secondly, that the trouble is not the absence of experiences, but their defective and wrong character — wrong and defective from the standpoint of connection with further experience. The positive side of this point is even more important in connection with progressive education. It is not enough to insist upon the necessity of experience, nor even of activity in experience. Everything depends upon the *quality* of the experience which is had. The quality of any experience has two aspects. There is an immediate aspect of agreeableness or disagreeableness, and there is its influence upon later experiences. The first is obvious and easy to judge. The *effect* of an experience is not borne on its face. It sets a problem to the educator. It is his business to arrange for the kind of experiences which, while they do not repel the student, but rather engage his activities are, nevertheless, more than immediately enjoyable since they promote having desirable future experiences. Just as no man lives or dies to himself, so no experience lives and dies to itself. Wholly independent of desire or intent, every experience lives on in further experiences. Hence the central problem of an education based upon experience is to select the kind of present experiences that live fruitfully and creatively in subsequent experiences.

Later, I shall discuss in more detail the principle of the continuity of

Chapter 2 The Need of a Theory of Experience

experience or what may be called the experiential continuum. Here I wish simply to emphasize the importance of this principle for the philosophy of educative experience. A philosophy of education, like any theory, has to be stated in words, in symbols. But so far as it is more than verbal it is a plan for conducting education. Like any plan, it must be framed with reference to what is to be done and how it is to be done. The more definitely and sincerely it is held that education is a development within, by, and for experience, the more important it is that there shall be clear conceptions of what experience is. Unless experience is so conceived that the result is a plan for deciding upon subject-matter, upon methods of instruction and discipline, and upon material equipment and social organization of the school, it is wholly in the air. It is reduced to a form of words which may be emotionally stirring but for which any other set of words might equally well be substituted unless they indicate operations to be initiated and executed. Just because traditional education was a matter of routine in which the plans and programs were handed down from the past, it does not follow that progressive education is a matter of planless improvisation.

The traditional school could get along without any consistently developed philosophy of education. About all it required in that line was a set of abstract words like culture, discipline, our great cultural heritage, etc., actual guidance being derived not from them but from custom and established routines. Just because progressive schools cannot rely upon established traditions and institutional habits, they must either proceed more or less haphazardly or be directed by ideas which, when they are made articulate and coherent, form a philosophy of education. Revolt against the kind of organization characteristic of the traditional school constitutes a demand for a kind of organization based upon ideas. I think that only slight acquaintance with the history of education is needed to prove that educational reformers and innovators alone have felt the need for a philosophy of education. Those who adhered to the established system needed merely a few fine-sounding words to justify existing practices. The real work was done by habits which were so fixed as to be institutional. The lesson for progressive education is that it requires in an urgent degree, a degree more pressing than was incumbent upon former innovators, a philosophy of education based upon a philosophy of experience.

I remarked incidentally that the philosophy in question is, to paraphrase the saying of Lincoln about democracy, one of education of, by, and for experience. No one of these words, *of, by,* or *for*, names anything which is self-evident. Each of them is a challenge to discover and put into operation a principle of order and organization which follows from understanding what educative experience signifies.

Chapter 2 The Need of a Theory of Experience

It is, accordingly, a much more difficult task to work out the kinds of materials, of methods, and of social relationships that are appropriate to the new education than is the case with traditional education. I think many of the difficulties experienced in the conduct of progressive schools and many of the criticisms leveled against them arise from this source. The difficulties are aggravated and the criticisms are increased when it is supposed that the new education is somehow easier than the old. This belief is, I imagine, more or less current. Perhaps it illustrates again the *Either-Or* philosophy, springing from the idea that about all which is required is *not* to do what is done in traditional schools.

I admit gladly that the new education is *simpler* in principle than the old. It is in harmony with principles of growth, while there is very much which is artificial in the old selection and arrangement of subjects and methods, and artificiality always leads to unnecessary complexity. But the easy and the simple are not identical. To discover what is really simple and to act upon the discovery is an exceedingly difficult task. After the artificial and complex is once institutionally established and ingrained in custom and routine, it is easier to walk in the paths that have been beaten than it is, after taking a new point of view, to work out what is practically involved in the new point of view. The old Ptolemaic astronomical system was more complicated with its cycles and epicycles than the Copernican system. But until organization of actual astronomical phenomena on the ground of the latter principle had been effected the easiest course was to follow the line of least resistance provided by the old intellectual habit. So we come back to the idea that a coherent *theory* of experience, affording positive direction to selection and organization of appropriate educational methods and materials, is required by the attempt to give new direction to the work of the schools. The process is a slow and arduous one. It is a matter of growth, and there are many obstacles which tend to obstruct growth and to deflect it into wrong lines.

I shall have something to say later about organization. All that is needed, perhaps, at this point is to say that we must escape from the tendency to think of organization in terms of the *kind* of organization, whether of content (or subject-matter), or of methods and social relations, that mark traditional education. I think that a good deal of the current opposition to the idea of organization is due to the fact that it is so hard to get away from the picture of the studies of the old school. The moment "organization" is mentioned imagination goes almost automatically to the kind of organization that is familiar, and in revolting against that we are led to shrink from the very idea of any organization. On the other hand, educational reactionaries, who are now gathering force, use the absence of adequate intellectual and moral organization in the newer type of school as proof not only of the need of organization, but to identify any and every kind

Chapter 2 The Need of a Theory of Experience

of organization with that instituted before the rise of experimental science. Failure to develop a conception of organization upon the empirical and experimental basis gives reactionaries a too easy victory. But the fact that the empirical sciences now offer the best type of intellectual organization which can be found in any field shows that there is no reason why we, who call ourselves emipiricists, should be "pushovers" in the matter of order and organization.

CHAPTER 3

CRITERIA OF EXPERIENCE

If there is any truth in what has been said about the need of forming a theory of experience in order that education may be intelligently conducted upon the basis of experience, it is clear that the next thing in order in this discussion is to present the principles that are most significant in framing this theory. I shall not, therefore, apologize for engaging in a certain amount of philosophical analysis, which otherwise might be out of place. I may, however, reassure you to some degree by saying that this analysis is not an end in itself but is engaged in for the sake of obtaining criteria to be applied later in discussion of a number of concrete and, to most persons, more interesting issues.

I have already mentioned what I called the category of continuity, or the experiential continuum. This principle is involved, as I pointed out, in every attempt to discriminate between experiences that are worth while educationally and those that are not. It may seem superfluous to argue that this discrimination is necessary not only in criticizing the traditional type of education but also in initiating and conducting a different type. Nevertheless, it is advisable to pursue for a little while the idea that it is necessary. One may safely assume, I suppose, that one thing which has recommended the progressive movement is that it seems more in accord with the democratic ideal to which our people is committed than do the procedures of the traditional school, since the latter have so much of the autocratic about them. Another thing which has contributed to its favorable reception is that its methods are humane in comparison with the harshness so often attending the policies of the traditional school.

The question I would raise concerns why we prefer democratic and humane arrangements to those which are autocratic and harsh. And by "why," I mean the *reason* for preferring them, not just the *causes* which lead us to the preference. One *cause* may be that we have been taught not only in the schools but by the press, the pulpit, the platform, and our laws and law-making bodies that democracy is the best of all social institutions. We may have so assimilated this idea from our surroundings that it has become an habitual part of our mental and moral make-up. But similar causes have led other persons in different surroundings to widely varying conclusions — to prefer

Chapter 3 Criteria of Experience

fascism, for example. The cause for our preference is not the same thing as the reason why we *should* prefer it.

It is not my purpose here to go in detail into the reason. But I would ask a single question: Can we find any reason that does not ultimately come down to the belief that democratic social arrangements promote a better quality of human experience, one which is more widely accessible and enjoyed, than do non-democratic and anti-democratic forms of social life? Does not the principle of regard for individual freedom and for decency and kindliness of human relations come back in the end to the conviction that these things are tributary to a higher quality of experience on the part of a greater number than are methods of repression and coercion or force? Is it not the reason for our preference that we believe that mutual consultation and convictions reached through persuasion, make possible a better quality of experience than can otherwise be provided on any wide scale?

If the answer to these questions is in the affirmative (and personally I do not see how we can justify our preference for democracy and humanity on any other ground), the ultimate reason for hospitality to progressive education, because of its reliance upon and use of humane methods and its kinship to democracy, goes back to the fact that discrimination is made between the inherent values of different experiences. So I come back to the principle of continuity of experience as a criterion of discrimination.

At bottom, this principle rests upon the fact of habit, when *habit* is interpreted biologically. The basic characteristic of habit is that every experience enacted and undergone modifies the one who acts and undergoes, while this modification affects, whether we wish it or not, the quality of subsequent experiences. For it is a somewhat different person who enters into them. The principle of habit so understood obviously goes deeper than the ordinary conception of *a* habit as a more or less fixed way of doing things, although it includes the latter as one of its special cases. It covers the formation of attitudes, attitudes that are emotional and intellectual; it covers our basic sensitivities and ways of meeting and responding to all the conditions which we meet in living. From this point of view, the principle of continuity of experience means that every experience both takes up something from those which have gone before and modifies in some way the quality of those which come after. As the poet states it,

...all experience is an arch wherethro'
Gleams that untraveled world, whose margin fades
For ever and for ever when I move.

So far, however, we have no ground for discrimination among

Chapter 3 Criteria of Experience

experiences. For the principle is of universal application. There is *some* kind of continuity in every case. It is when we note the different forms in which continuity of experience operates that we get the basis of discriminating among experiences. I may illustrate what is meant by an objection which has been brought against an idea which I once put forth — namely, that the educative process can be identified with growth when that is understood in terms of the active participle, *growing*.

Growth, or growing as developing, not only physically but intellectually and morally, is one exemplification of the principle of continuity. The objection made is that growth might take many different directions: a man, for example, who starts out on a career of burglary may grow in that direction, and by practice may grow into a highly expert burglar. Hence it is argued that "growth" is not enough; we must also specify the direction in which growth takes place, the end towards which it tends. Before, however, we decide that the objection is conclusive we must analyze the case a little further.

That a man may grow in efficiency as a burglar, as a gangster, or as a corrupt politician, cannot be doubted. But from the standpoint of growth as education and education as growth the question is whether growth in this direction promotes or retards growth in general. Does this form of growth create conditions for further growth, or does it set up conditions that shut off the person who has grown in this particular direction from the occasions, stimuli, and opportunities for continuing growth in new directions? What is the effect of growth in a special direction upon the attitudes and habits which alone open up avenues for development in other lines? I shall leave you to answer these questions, saying simply that when and *only* when development in a particular line conduces to continuing growth does it answer to the criterion of education as growing. For the conception is one that must find universal and not specialized limited application.

I return now to the question of continuity as a criterion by which to discriminate between experiences which are educative and those which are mis-educative. As we have seen, there is some kind of continuity in any case since every experience affects for better or worse the attitudes which help decide the quality of further experiences, by setting up certain preference and aversion, and making it easier or harder to act for this or that end. Moreover, every experience influences in some degree the objective conditions under which further experiences are had. For example, a child who learns to speak has a new facility and new desire. But he has also widened the external conditions of subsequent learning. When he learns to read, he similarly opens up a new environment. If a person decides to become a teacher, lawyer, physician, or stockbroker, when he executes his intention he thereby necessarily determines to some

Chapter 3 Criteria of Experience

extent the environment in which he will act in the future. He has rendered himself more sensitive and responsive to certain conditions, and relatively immune to those things about him that would have been stimuli if he had made another choice.

But, while the principle of continuity applies in some way in every case, the quality of the present experience influences the *way* in which the principle applies. We speak of spoiling a child and of the spoilt child, the effect of over-indulging a child is a continuing one. It sets up an attitude which operates as an automatic demand that persons and objects cater to his desires and caprices in the future. It makes him seek the kind of situation that will enable him to do what he feels like doing at the time. It renders him averse to and comparatively incompetent in situations which require effort and perseverance in overcoming obstacles. There is no paradox in the fact that the principle of the continuity of experience may operate so as to leave a person arrested on a low plane of development, in a way which limits later capacity for growth.

On the other hand, if an experience arouses curiosity, strengthens initiative, and sets up desires and purposes that are sufficiently intense to carry a person over dead places in the future, continuity works in a very different way. Every experience is a moving force. Its value can be judged only on the ground of what it moves toward and into. The greater maturity of experience which should belong to the adult as educator puts him in a position to evaluate each experience of the young in a way in which the one having the less mature experience cannot do. It is then the business of the educator to see in what direction an experience is heading. There is no point in his being more mature if, instead of using his greater insight to help organize the conditions of the experience of the immature, he throws away his insight. Failure to take the moving force of an experience into account so as to judge and direct it on the ground of what it is moving into means disloyalty to the principle of experience itself. The disloyalty operates in two directions. The educator is false to the understanding that he should have obtained from his own past experience. He is also unfaithful to the fact that all human experience is ultimately social: that it involves contact and communication. The mature person, to put it in moral terms, has no right to withhold from the young on given occasions whatever capacity for sympathetic understanding his own experience has given him.

No sooner, however, are such things said than there is a tendency to react to the other extreme and take what has been said as a plea for some sort of disguised imposition from outside. It is worth while, accordingly, to say something about the way in which the adult can exercise the wisdom his own wider experience gives him without imposing a merely external control. On one side, it is his business

Chapter 3 Criteria of Experience

to be on the alert to see what attitudes and habitual tendencies are being created. In this direction he must, if he is an educator, be able to judge what attitudes are actually conducive to continued growth and what are detrimental. He must, in addition, have that sympathetic understanding of individuals as individuals which gives him an idea of what is actually going on in the minds of those who are learning. It is, among other things, the need for these abilities on the part of the parent and teacher which makes a system of education based upon living experience a more difficult affair to conduct successfully than it is to follow the patterns of traditional education.

But there is another aspect of the matter. Experience does not go on simply inside a person. It does go on there, for it influences the formation of attitudes of desire and purpose. But this is not the whole of the story. Every genuine experience has an active side which changes in some degree the objective conditions under which experiences are had. The difference between civilization and savagery, to take an example on a large scale, is found in the degree in which previous experiences have changed the objective conditions under which subsequent experiences take place. The existence of roads, of means of rapid movement and transportation, tools, implements, furniture, electric light and power, are illustrations. Destroy the external conditions of present civilized experience, and for a time our experience would relapse into that of barbaric peoples.

Experience and Education

In a word, we live from birth to death in a world of persons and things which in large measure is what it is because of what has been done and transmitted from previous human activities. When this fact is ignored, experience is treated as if it were something which goes on exclusively inside an individual's body and mind. It ought not to be necessary to say that experience does not occur in a vacuum. There are sources outside an individual which give rise to experience. It is constantly fed from these springs. No one would question that a child in a slum tenement has a different experience from that of a child in a cultured home; that the country lad has a different kind of experience from the city boy, or a boy on the seashore one different from the lad who is brought up on inland prairies. Ordinarily we take such facts for granted as too commonplace to record. But when their educational import is recognized, they indicate the second way in which the educator can direct the experience of the young without engaging in imposition. A primary responsibility of educators is that they not only be aware of the general principle of the shaping of actual experience by environing conditions, but that they also recognize in the concrete what surroundings are conducive to having experiences that lead to growth. Above all, they should know how to utilize the surroundings, physical and social, that exist so as to extract from them all that they have to contribute to building up experiences that are worth while.

Traditional education did not have to face this problem; it could systematically dodge this responsibility. The school environment of desks, blackboards, a small school yard, was supposed to suffice. There was no demand that the teacher should become intimately acquainted with the conditions of the local community, physical, historical, economic, occupational, etc., in order to utilize them as educational resources. A system of education based upon the necessary connection of education with experience must, on the contrary, if faithful to its principle, take these things constantly into account. This tax upon the educator is another reason why progressive education is more difficult to carry on than was ever the traditional system.

It is possible to frame schemes of education that pretty systematically subordinate objective conditions to those which reside in the individuals being educated. This happens whenever the place and function of the teacher, of books, of apparatus and equipment, of everything which represents the products of the more mature experience of elders, is systematically subordinated to the immediate inclinations and feelings of the young. Every theory which assumes that importance can be attached to these objective factors only at the expense of imposing external control and of limiting the freedom of individuals rests finally upon the notion that experience is truly experience only when objective conditions are subordinated to what goes on within the individuals having the experience.

I do not mean that it is supposed that objective conditions can be shut out. It is recognized that they must enter in: so much concession is made to the inescapable fact that we live in a world of things and persons. But I think that observation of what goes on in some families and some schools would disclose that some parents and some teachers are acting upon the idea of *subordinating* objective conditions to internal ones. In that case, it is assumed not only that the latter are primary, which in one sense they are, but that just as they temporarily exist they fix the whole educational process.

Let me illustrate from the case of an infant. The needs of a baby for food, rest, and activity are certainly primary and decisive in one respect. Nourishment must be provided; provision must be made for comfortable sleep, and so on. But these facts do not mean that a parent shall feed the baby at any time when the baby is cross or irritable, that there shall not be a program of regular hours of feeding and sleeping, etc. The wise mother takes account of the needs of the infant but not in a way which dispenses with her own responsibility for regulating the objective conditions under which the needs are satisfied. And if she is a wise mother in this respect, she draws upon past experiences of experts as well as her own for the light that these shed upon what experiences are in general most conducive to the normal development of infants. Instead of these conditions being subordinated to the immediate internal condition of the baby, they are

Chapter 3 Criteria of Experience

definitely ordered so that a particular kind of *interaction* with these immediate internal states may be brought about.

The word "interaction," which has just been used, expresses the second chief principle for interpreting an experience in its educational function and force. It assigns equal rights to both factors in experience — objective and internal conditions. Any normal experience is an interplay of these two sets of conditions. Taken together, or in their interaction, they form what we call a *situation*. The trouble with traditional education was not that it emphasized the external conditions that enter into the control of the experiences but that it paid so little attention to the internal factors which also decide what kind of experience is had. It violated the principle of interaction from one side. But this violation is no reason why the new education should violate the principle from the other side — except upon the basis of the extreme *Either-Or* educational philosophy which has been mentioned.

The illustration drawn from the need for regulation of the objective conditions of a baby's development indicates, first, that the parent has responsibility for arranging the conditions under which an infant's experience of food, sleep, etc., occurs, and, secondly, that the responsibility is fulfilled by utilizing the funded experience of the past, as this is represented, say, by the advice of competent physicians and others who have made a special study of normal physical growth.

Does it limit the freedom of the mother when she uses the body of knowledge thus provided to regulate the objective conditions of nourishment and sleep? Or does the enlargement of her intelligence in fulfilling her parental function widen her freedom? Doubtless if a fetish were made of the advice and directions so that they came to be inflexible dictates to be followed under every possible condition, then restriction of freedom of both parent and child would occur. But this restriction would also be a limitation of the intelligence that is exercised in personal judgment.

In what respect does regulation of objective conditions limit the freedom of the baby? Some limitation is certainly placed upon its immediate movements and inclinations when it is put in its crib, at a time when it wants to continue playing, or does not get food at the moment it would like it, or when it isn't picked up and dandled when it cries for attention. Restriction also occurs when mother or nurse snatches a child away from an open fire into which it is about to fall. I shall have more to say later about freedom. Here it is enough to ask whether freedom is to be thought of and adjudged on the basis of relatively momentary incidents or whether its meaning is found in the continuity of developing experience.

The statement that individuals live in a world means, in the concrete, that they live in a series of situations. And when it is said that they live *in* these situations, the meaning of the word "in" is different from its meaning when it is said that pennies are "in" a pocket or paint is "in" a can. It means, once more, that interaction is going on between an individual and objects and other persons. The conceptions of *situation* and of *interaction* are inseparable from each other. An experience is always what it is because of a transaction taking place between an individual and what, at the time, constitutes his environment, whether the latter consists of persons with whom he is talking about some topic or event, the subject talked about being also a part of the situation; or the toys with which he is playing; the book he is reading (in which his environing conditions at the time may be England or ancient Greece or an imaginary region); or the materials of an experiment he is performing. The environment, in other words, is whatever conditions interact with personal needs, desires, purposes, and capacities to create the experience which is had. Even when a person builds a castle in the air he is interacting with the objects which he constructs in fancy.

The two principles of continuity and interaction are not separate from each other. They intercept and unite. They are, so to speak, the longitudinal and lateral aspects of experience. Different situations succeed one another. But because of the principle of continuity something is carried over from the earlier to the later ones. As an individual passes from one situation to another, his world, his environment, expands or contracts. He does not find himself living in another world but in a different part or aspect of one and the same world. What he has learned in the way of knowledge and skill in one situation becomes an instrument of understanding and dealing effectively with the situations which follow. The process goes on as long as life and learning continue. Otherwise the course of experience is disorderly, since the individual factor that enters into making an experience is split. A divided world, a world whose parts and aspects do not hang together, is at once a sign and a cause of a divided personality. When the splitting-up reaches a certain point we call the person insane. A fully integrated personality, on the other hand, exists only when successive experiences are integrated with one another. It can be built up only as a world of related objects is constructed.

Continuity and interaction in their active union with each other provide the measure of the educative significance and value of an experience. The immediate and direct concern of an educator is then with the situations in which interaction takes place. The individual, who enters as a factor into it, is what he is at a given time. It is the other factor, that of objective conditions, which lies to some extent within the possibility of regulation by the educator. As has already been noted, the phrase "objective conditions" covers a wide range. It includes what is done by the educator and the way in which it is done, not only words spoken but the tone of voice in which they are spoken. It includes equipment, books, apparatus, toys, games played. It includes the materials with which an individual interacts, and, most important of all, the total *social* set-up of the situations in which a person is engaged.

When it is said that the objective conditions are those which are within the power of the educator to regulate, it is meant, of course, that his ability to influence directly the experience of others and thereby the education they obtain places upon him the duty of determining that environment which will interact with the existing capacities and needs of those taught to create a worth-while experience. The trouble with traditional education was not that educators took upon themselves the responsibility for providing an environment. The trouble was that they did not consider the other factor in creating an experience; namely, the powers and purposes of those taught. It was assumed that a certain set of conditions was intrinsically desirable, apart from its ability to evoke a certain quality of response in individuals. This lack of mutual adaptation made the process of teaching and learning accidental. Those to whom the provided conditions were suitable managed to learn. Others got on as best they could. Responsibility for selecting objective conditions carries with it, then, the responsibility for understanding the needs and capacities of the individuals who are learning at a given time. It is not enough that certain materials and methods have proved effective with other individuals at other times. There must be a reason for thinking that they will function in generating an experience that has educative quality with particular individuals at a particular time.

It is no reflection upon the nutritive quality of beefsteak that it is not fed to infants. It is not an invidious reflection upon trigonometry that we do not teach it in the first or fifth grade of school. It is not the subject *per se* that is educative or that is conducive to growth. There is no subject that is in and of itself, or without regard to the stage of growth attained by the learner, such that inherent educational value can be attributed to it. Failure to take into account adaptation to the needs and capacities of individuals was the source of the idea that certain subjects and certain methods are intrinsically cultural or intrinsically good for mental discipline. There is no such thing as educational value in the abstract. The notion that some subjects and methods and that acquaintance with certain facts and truths possess educational value in and of themselves is the reason why traditional education reduced the material of education so largely to a diet of predigested materials. According to this notion, it was enough to regulate the quantity and difficulty of the material provided, in a scheme of quantitative grading, from month to month and from year to year. Otherwise a pupil was expected to take it in the doses that were prescribed from without. If the pupil left it instead of taking it, if he engaged in physical truancy, or in the mental truancy of mind-

Chapter 3 Criteria of Experience

wandering and finally built up an emotional revulsion against the subject, he was held to be at fault. No question was raised as to whether the trouble might not lie in the subject-matter or in the way in which it was offered. The principle of interaction makes it clear that failure of adaptation of material to needs and capacities of individuals may cause an experience to be non-educative quite as much as failure of an individual to adapt himself to the material.

The principle of continuity in its educational application means, nevertheless, that the future has to be taken into account at every stage of the educational process. This idea is easily misunderstood and is badly distorted in traditional education. Its assumption is, that by acquiring certain skills and by learning certain subjects which would be needed later (perhaps in college or perhaps in adult life) pupils are as a matter of course made ready for the needs and circumstances of the future. Now "preparation" is a treacherous idea. In a certain sense every experience should do something to prepare a person for later experiences of a deeper and more expansive quality. That is the very meaning of growth, continuity, reconstruction of experience. But it is a mistake to suppose that the mere acquisition of a certain amount of arithmetic, geography, history, etc., which is taught and studied because it may be useful at some time in the future, has this effect, and it is a mistake to suppose that acquisition of skills in reading and figuring will automatically constitute preparation for their right and effective use under conditions very unlike those in which they were acquired.

Almost everyone has had occasion to look back upon his school days and wonder what has become of the knowledge he was supposed to have amassed during his years of schooling, and why it is that the technical skills he acquired have to be learned over again in changed form in order to stand him in good stead. Indeed, he is lucky who does not find that in order to make progress, in order to go ahead intellectually, he does not have to unlearn much of what he learned in school. These questions cannot be disposed of by saying that the subjects were not actually learned, for they were learned at least sufficiently to enable a pupil to pass examinations in them. One trouble is that the subject-matter in question was learned in isolation; it was put, as it were, in a water-tight compartment. When the question is asked, then, what has become of it, where has it gone to, the right answer is that it is still there in the special compartment in which it was originally stowed away. If exactly the same conditions recurred as those under which it was acquired, it would also recur and be available. But it was segregated when it was acquired and hence is so disconnected from the rest of experience that it is not available under the actual conditions of life. It is contrary to the laws of experience that learning of this kind, no matter how thoroughly engrained at the time, should give genuine preparation.

Nor does failure in preparation end at this point. Perhaps the greatest of all pedagogical fallacies is the notion that a person learns only the particular thing he is studying at the time. Collateral learning in the way of formation of enduring attitudes, of likes and dislikes, may be and often is much more important than the spelling lesson or lesson in geography or history that is learned. For these attitudes are fundamentally what count in the future. The most important attitude that can be formed is that of desire to go on learning. If impetus in this direction is weakened instead of being intensified, something much more than mere lack of preparation takes place. The pupil is actually robbed of native capacities which otherwise would enable him to cope with the circumstances that he meets in the course of his life. We often see persons who have had little schooling and in whose case the absence of set schooling proves to be a positive asset. They have at least retained their native common sense and power of judgment, and its exercise in the actual conditions of living has given them the precious gift of ability to learn from the experiences they have. What avail is it to win prescribed amounts of information about geography and history, to win ability to read and write, if in the process the individual loses his own soul: loses his appreciation of things worth while, of the values to which these things are relative; if he loses desire to apply what he has learned and, above all, loses the ability to extract meaning from his future experiences as they occur?

What, then, is the true meaning of preparation in the educational scheme? In the first place, it means that a person, young or old, gets out of his present experience all that there is in it for him at the time in which he has it. When preparation is made the controlling end, then the potentialities of the present are sacrificed to a suppositious future. When this happens, the actual preparation for the future is missed or distorted. The ideal of using the present simply to get ready for the future contradicts itself. It omits, and even shuts out, the very conditions by which a person can be prepared for his future. We always live at the time we live and not at some other time, and only by extracting at each present time the full meaning of each present experience are we prepared for doing the same thing in the future. This is the only preparation which in the long run amounts to anything.

All this means that attentive care must be devoted to the conditions which give each present experience a worthwhile meaning. Instead of inferring that it doesn't make much difference what the present experience is as long as it is enjoyed, the conclusion is the exact opposite. Here is another matter where it is easy to react from one extreme to the other. Because traditional schools tended to sacrifice the present to a remote and more or less unknown future, therefore it comes to be believed that the educator has little responsibility for the kind of present experiences the young undergo. But the relation of the present and the future is not an *Either-Or* affair. The present affects the future anyway. The persons who should have some idea of the connection between the two are those who have achieved maturity. Accordingly, upon them devolves the responsibility for instituting the conditions for the kind of present experience which has a favorable effect upon the future. Education as growth or maturity should be an ever-present process.

CHAPTER 4

SOCIAL CONTROL

I have said that educational plans and projects, seeing education in terms of life-experience, are thereby committed to framing and adopting an intelligent theory or, if you please, philosophy of experience. Otherwise they are at the mercy of every intellectual breeze that happens to blow. I have tried to illustrate the need for such a theory by calling attention to two principles which are fundamental in the constitution of experience: the principles of interaction and of continuity. If, then, I am asked why I have spent so much time on expounding a rather abstract philosophy, it is because practical attempts to develop schools based upon the idea that education is found in life-experience are bound to exhibit inconsistencies and confusions unless they are guided by some conception of what experience is, and what marks off educative experience from non-educative and mis-educative experience. I now come to a group of actual educational questions the discussion of which will, I hope, provide topics and material that are more concrete than the discussion up to this point.

The two principles of continuity and interaction as criteria of the value of experience are so intimately connected that it is not easy to tell just what special educational problem to take up first. Even the convenient division into problems of subject-matter or studies and of methods of teaching and learning is likely to fail us in selection and organization of topics to discuss. Consequently, the beginning and sequence of topics is somewhat arbitrary. I shall commence, however, with the old question of individual freedom and social control and pass on to the questions that grow naturally out of it.

It is often well in considering educational problems to get a start by temporarily ignoring the school and thinking of other human situations. I take it that no one would deny that the ordinary good citizen is as a matter of fact subject to a great deal of social control and that a considerable part of this control is not felt to involve restriction of personal freedom. Even the theoretical anarchist, whose philosophy commits him to the idea that state or government control is an unmitigated evil, believes that with abolition of the political state other forms of social control would operate: indeed, his opposition to governmental regulation springs from his belief that other and to him more normal modes of control would operate with abolition of the state.

Without taking up this extreme position, let us note some examples of social control that operate in everyday life, and then look for the principle underlying them. Let us begin with the young people themselves. Children at recess or after school play games, from tag and one-old-cat to baseball and football. The games involve rules, and these rules order their conduct. The games do not go on haphazardly or by a succession of improvisations. Without rules there is no game. If disputes arise there is an umpire to appeal to, or discussion and a kind of arbitration are means to a decision; otherwise the game is broken up and comes to an end.

There are certain fairly obvious controlling features of such situations to which I want to call attention. The first is that the rules are a part of the game. They are not outside of it. No rules, then no game; different rules, then a different game. As long as the game goes on with a reasonable smoothness, the players do not feel that they are submitting to external imposition but that they are playing the game. In the second place an individual may at times feel that a decision isn't fair and he may even get angry. But he is not objecting to a rule but to what he claims is a violation of it, to some one-sided and unfair action. In the third place, the rules, and hence the conduct of the game, are fairly standardized. There are recognized ways of counting out, of selection of sides, as well as for positions to be taken, movements to be made, etc. These rules have the sanction of tradition and precedent. Those playing the game have seen, perhaps, professional matches and they want to emulate their elders. An element that is conventional is pretty strong. Usually, a group of youngsters change the rides by which they play only when the adult group to which they look for models have themselves made a change in the rules, while the change made by the elders is at least supposed to conduce to making the game more skillful or more interesting to spectators.

Now, the general conclusion I would draw is that control of individual actions is effected by the whole situation in which individuals are involved, in which they share and of which they are co-operative or interacting parts. For even in a competitive game there is a certain kind of participation, of sharing in a common experience. Stated the other way around, those who take part do not feel that they are bossed by an individual person or are being subjected to the will of some outside superior person. When violent disputes do arise, it is usually on the alleged ground that the umpire or some person on the other side is being unfair; in other words, that in such cases some individual is trying to impose his individual will on someone else.

It may seem to be putting too heavy a load upon a single case

Chapter 4 Social Control

to argue that this instance illustrates the general principle of social control of individuals without the violation of freedom. But if the matter were followed out through a number of cases, I think the conclusion that this particular instance does illustrate a general principle would be justified. Games are generally competitive. If we took instances of co-operative activities in which all members of a group take part, as for example in well-ordered family life in which there is mutual confidence, the point would be even clearer. In all such cases it is not the will or desire of any one person which establishes order but the moving spirit of the whole group. The control is social, but individuals are parts of a community, not outside of it.

I do not mean by this that there are no occasions upon which the authority of, say, the parent does not have to intervene and exercise fairly direct control. But I do say that, in the first place, the number of these occasions is slight in comparison with the number of those in which the control is exercised by situations in which all take part. And what is even more important, the authority in question when exercised in a well-regulated household or other community group is not a manifestation of merely personal will; the parent or teacher exercises it as the representative and agent of the interests of the group as a whole. With respect to the first point, in a well-ordered school the main reliance for control of this and that individual is upon the activities carried on and upon the situations in which these activities are maintained. The teacher reduces to a minimum the occasions in which he or she has to exercise authority in a personal way. When it is necessary, in the second place, to speak and act firmly, it is done in behalf of the interest of the group, not as an exhibition of personal power. This makes the difference between action which is arbitrary and that which is just and fair.

Moreover, it is not necessary that the difference should be formulated in words, by either teacher or the young, in order to be felt in experience. The number of children who do not feel the difference (even if they cannot articulate it and reduce it to an intellectual principle) between action that is motivated by personal power and desire to dictate and action that is fair, because in the interest of all, is small. I should even be willing to say that upon the whole children are more sensitive to the signs and symptoms of this difference than are adults. Children learn the difference when playing with one another. They are willing, often too willing if anything, to take suggestions from one child and let him be a leader if his conduct adds to the experienced value of what they are doing, while they resent the attempt at dictation. Then they often withdraw and when asked why, say that it is because so-and-so "is too bossy."

I do not wish to refer to the traditional school in ways which set up a caricature in lieu of a picture. But I think it is fair to say that one

Chapter 4 Social Control

reason the personal commands of the teacher so often played an undue role and a season why the order which existed was so much a matter of sheer obedience to the will of an adult was because the situation almost forced it upon the teacher. The school was not a group or community held together by participation in common activities. Consequently, the normal, proper conditions of control were lacking. Their absence was made up for, and to a considerable extent had to be made up for, by the direct intervention of the teacher, who, as the saying went, "*kept* order." He kept it because order was in the teacher's keeping, instead of residing in the shared work being done.

The conclusion is that in what are called the new schools, the primary source of social control resides in the very nature of the work done as a social enterprise in which all individuals have an opportunity to contribute and to which all feel a responsibility. Most children are naturally "sociable." Isolation is even more irksome to them than to adults. A genuine community life has its ground in this natural sociability. But community life does not organize itself in an enduring way purely spontaneously. It requires thought and planning ahead. The educator is responsible for a knowledge of individuals and for a knowledge of subject-matter that will enable activities to be selected which lend themselves to social organization, an organization in which all individuals have an opportunity to contribute something, and in which the activities in which all participate are the chief carrier of control.

I am not romantic enough about the young to suppose that every pupil will respond or that any child of normally strong impulses will respond on every occasion. There are likely to be some who, when they come to school, are already victims of injurious conditions outside of the school and who have become so passive and unduly docile that they fail to contribute. There will be others who, because of previous experience, are bumptious and unruly and perhaps downright rebellious. But it is certain that the general principle of social control cannot be predicated upon such cases. It is also true that no general rule can be laid down for dealing with such cases. The teacher has to deal with them individually. They fall into general classes, but no two are exactly alike. The educator has to discover as best he or she can the causes for the recalcitrant attitudes. He or she cannot, if the educational process is to go on, make it a question of pitting one will against another in order to see which is strongest, nor yet allow the unruly and non-participating pupils to stand permanently in the way of the educative activities of others. Exclusion perhaps is the only available measure at a given juncture, but it is no solution. For it may strengthen the very causes which have brought about the undesirable anti-social attitude, such as desire for attention or to show off.

Chapter 4 Social Control

Exceptions rarely prove a rule or give a clew to what the rule should be. I would not, therefore, attach too much importance to these exceptional cases, although it is true at present that progressive schools are likely often to have more than their fair share of these cases, since parents may send children to such schools as a last resort. I do not think weakness in control when it is found in progressive schools arises in any event from these exceptional cases. It is much more likely to arise from failure to arrange in advance for the kind of work (by which I mean all kinds of activities engaged in) which will create situations that of themselves tend to exercise control over what this, that, and the other pupil does and how he does it. This failure most often goes back to lack of sufficiently thoughtful planning in advance. The causes for such lack are varied. The one which is peculiarly important to mention in this connection is the idea that such advance planning is unnecessary and even that it is inherently hostile to the legitimate freedom of those being instructed.

Now, of course, it is quite possible to have preparatory planning by the teacher done in such a rigid and intellectually inflexible fashion that it does result in adult imposition, which is none the less external because executed with tact and the semblance of respect for individual freedom. But this kind of planning does not follow inherently from the principle involved. I do not know what the greater maturity of the teacher and the teacher's greater knowledge of the world, of subject-matters and of individuals, is for unless the teacher can arrange conditions that are conducive to community activity and to organization which exercises control over individual impulses by the mere fact that all are engaged in communal projects. Because the kind of advance planning heretofore engaged in has been so routine as to leave little room for the free play of individual thinking or for contributions due to distinctive individual experience, it does not follow that all planning must be rejected. On the contrary, there is incumbent upon the educator the duty of instituting a much more intelligent, and consequently more difficult, kind of planning. He must survey the capacities and needs of the particular set of individuals with whom he is dealing and must at the same time arrange the conditions which provide the subject-matter or content for experiences that satisfy these needs and develop these capacities. The planning must be flexible enough to permit free play for individuality of experience and yet firm enough to give direction towards continuous development of power.

The present occasion is a suitable one to say something about the province and office of the teacher. The principle that development of experience comes about through interaction means that education is essentially a social process. This quality is realized in the degree in which individuals form a community group. It is absurd to exclude the teacher from membership in the group. As the most mature member of the group he has a peculiar responsibility for the conduct of the interactions and intercommunications which are the very life of the group as a community. That children are individuals whose freedom should be respected while the more mature person should have no freedom as an individual is an idea too absurd to require refutation. The tendency to exclude the teacher from a positive and leading share in the direction of the activities of the community of which he is a member is another instance of reaction from one extreme to another. When pupils were a class rather than a social group, the teacher necessarily acted largely from the outside, not as a director of processes of exchange in which all had a share. When education is based upon experience and educative experience is seen to be a social process, the situation changes radically. The teacher loses the position of external boss or dictator but takes on that of leader of group activities.

In discussing the conduct of games as an example of normal social control, reference was made to the presence of a standardized conventional factor. The counterpart of this factor in school life is found in the question of manners, especially of good manners in the manifestations of politeness and courtesy. The more we know about customs in different parts of the world at different times in the history of mankind, the more we learn how much manners differ from place to place and time to time. This fact proves that there is a large conventional factor involved. But there is no group at any time or place which does not have some code of manners as, for example, with respect to proper ways of greeting other persons. The particular form a convention takes has nothing fixed and absolute about it. But the existence of some form of convention is not itself a convention. It is a uniform attendant of all social relationships. At the very least, it is the oil which prevents or reduces friction.

It is possible, of course, for these social forms to become, as we say, "mere formalities." They may become merely outward show with no meaning behind them. But the avoidance of empty ritualistic forms of social intercourse does not mean the rejection of every formal element. It rather indicates the need for development of forms of intercourse that are inherently appropriate to social situations. Visitors to some progressive schools are shocked by the lack of manners they come across. One who knows the situation better is aware that to some extent their absence is due to the eager interest of children to go on with what they are doing. In their eagerness they may, for example, bump into each other and into visitors with no word of apology. One might say that this condition is better than a display of merely external punctilio accompanying intellectual and emotional lack of interest in school work. But it also represents a failure in education, a failure to learn one of the most important lessons of life, that of mutual accommodation and adaptation. Education is going on

Chapter 4　Social Control

in a one-sided way, for attitudes and habits are in process of formation that stand in the way of the future learning that springs from easy and ready contact and communication with others.

CHAPTER 5

THE NATURE OF FREEDOM

At the risk of repeating what has been often said by me I want to say something about the other side of the problem of social control, namely, the nature of freedom. The only freedom that is of enduring importance is freedom of intelligence, that is to say, freedom of observation and of judgment exercised in behalf of purposes that are intrinsically worth while. The commonest mistake made about freedom is, I think, to identify it with freedom of movement, or with the external or physical side of activity. Now, this external and physical side of activity cannot be separated from the internal side of activity; from freedom of thought, desire, and purpose. The limitation that was put upon outward action by the fixed arrangements of the typical traditional schoolroom, with its fixed rows of desks and its military regimen of pupils who were permitted to move only at certain fixed signals, put a great restriction upon intellectual and moral freedom.

Straitjacket and chain-gang procedures had to be done away with if there was to be a chance for growth of individuals in the intellectual springs of freedom without which there is no assurance of genuine and continued normal growth.

But the fact still remains that an increased measure of freedom of outer movement is a *means*, not an end. The educational problem is not solved when this aspect of freedom is obtained. Everything then depends, so far as education is concerned, upon what is done with this added liberty. What end does it serve? What consequences flow from it? Let me speak first of the advantages which reside potentially in increase of outward freedom. In the first place, without its existence it is practically impossible for a teacher to gain knowledge of the individuals with whom he is concerned. Enforced quiet and acquiescence prevent pupils from disclosing their real natures. They enforce artificial uniformity. They put seeming before being. They place a premium upon preserving the outward appearance of attention, decorum, and obedience. And everyone who is acquainted with schools in which this system prevailed well knows that thoughts, imaginations, desires, and sly activities ran their own unchecked course behind this facade. They were disclosed to the teacher only when some untoward act led to their detection. One has only to contrast this highly artificial situation with normal human relations outside the schoolroom, say in a well-conducted home, to appreciate how fatal it is to the teacher's

Chapter 5　The Nature of Freedom

acquaintance with and understanding of the individuals who are, supposedly, being educated. Yet without this insight there is only an accidental chance that the material of study and the methods used in instruction will so come home to an individual that his development of mind and character is actually directed. There is a vicious circle. Mechanical uniformity of studies and methods creates a kind of uniform immobility and this reacts to perpetuate uniformity of studies and of recitations, while behind this enforced uniformity individual tendencies operate in irregular and more or less forbidden ways.

The other important advantage of increased outward freedom is found in the very nature of the learning process. That the older methods set a premium upon passivity and receptivity has been pointed out. Physical quiescence puts a tremendous premium upon these traits. The only escape from them in the standardized school is an activity which is irregular and perhaps disobedient. There cannot be complete quietude in a laboratory or workshop. The non-social character of the traditional school is seen in the fact that it erected silence into one of its prime virtues. There is, of course, such a thing as intense intellectual activity without overt bodily activity. But capacity for such intellectual activity marks a comparatively late achievement when it is continued for a long period. There should be brief intervals of time for quiet reflection provided for even the young. But they are periods of genuine reflection only when they follow after times of more overt action and are used to organize what has been gained in periods of activity in which the hands and other parts of the body beside the brain are used. Freedom of movement is also important as a means of maintaining normal physical and mental health. We have still to learn from the example of the Greeks who saw clearly the relation between a sound body and a sound mind. But in all the respects mentioned freedom of outward action is a means to freedom of judgment and of power to carry deliberately chosen ends into execution. The amount of external freedom which is needed varies from individual to individual. It naturally tends to decrease with increasing maturity, though its complete absence prevents even a mature individual from having the contacts which will provide him with new materials upon which his intelligence may exercise itself. The amount and the quality of this kind of free activity as a means of growth is a problem that must engage the thought of the educator at every stage of development.

There can be no greater mistake, however, than to treat such freedom as an end in itself. It then tends to be destructive of the shared cooperative activities which are the normal source of order. But, on the other hand, it turns freedom which should be positive into something negative. For freedom from restriction, the negative side, is to be prized only as a means to a freedom which is power: power to frame purposes, to judge wisely, to evaluate desires by the

Chapter 5 The Nature of Freedom

consequences which will result from acting upon them; power to select and order means to carry chosen ends into operation.

Natural impulses and desires constitute in any case the starting point. But there is no intellectual growth without some reconstruction, some remaking, of impulses and desires in the form in which they first show themselves. This remaking involves inhibition of impulse in its first estate. The alternative to externally imposed inhibition is inhibition through an individual's own reflection and judgment. The old phrase "stop and think" is sound psychology. For thinking is stoppage of the immediate manifestation of impulse until that impulse has been brought into connection with other possible tendencies to action so that a more comprehensive and coherent plan of activity is formed. Some of the other tendencies to action lead to use of eye, ear, and hand to observe objective conditions; others result in recall of what has happened in the past. Thinking is thus a postponement of immediate action, while it effects internal control of impulse through a union of observation and memory, this union being the heart of reflection. What has been said explains the meaning of the well-worn phrase "self-control." The ideal aim of education is creation of power of self-control. But the mere removal of external control is no guarantee for the production of self-control. It is easy to jump out of the frying-pan into the fire. It is easy, in other words, to escape one form of external control only to find oneself in another and more dangerous form of external control. Impulses and desires that are not ordered by intelligence are under the control of accidental circumstances. It may be a loss rather than a gain to escape from the control of another person only to find one's conduct dictated by immediate whim and caprice; that is, at the mercy of impulses into whose formation intelligent judgment has not entered. A person whose conduct is controlled in this way has at most only the illusion of freedom. Actually he is directed by forces over which he has no command.

CHAPTER 6

THE MEANING OF PURPOSE

It is, then, a sound instinct which identifies freedom with power to frame purposes and to execute or carry into effect purposes so framed. Such freedom is in turn identical with self-control; for the formation of purposes and the organization of means to execute them are the work of intelligence. Plato once defined a slave as the person who executes the purposes of another, and, as has just been said, a person is also a slave who is enslaved to his own blind desires. There is, I think, no point in the philosophy of progressive education which is sounder than its emphasis upon the importance of the participation of the learner in the formation of the purposes which direct his activities in the learning process, just as there is no defect in traditional education greater than its failure to secure the active co-operation of the pupil in construction of the purposes involved in his studying. But the meaning of purposes and ends is not self-evident and self-explanatory. The more their educational importance is emphasized, the more important it is to understand what a purpose is; how it arises and how it functions in experience.

A genuine purpose always starts with an impulse. Obstruction of the immediate execution of an impulse converts it into a desire. Nevertheless neither impulse nor desire is itself a purpose. A purpose is an end-view. That is, it involves foresight of the consequences which will result from acting upon impulse. Foresight of consequences involves the operation of intelligence. It demands, in the first place, observation of objective conditions and circumstances. For impulse and desire produce consequences not by themselves alone but through their interaction or co-operation with surrounding conditions. The impulse for such a simple action as walking is executed only in active conjunction with the ground on which one stands. Under ordinary circumstances, we do not have to pay much attention to the ground. In a ticklish situation we have to observe very carefully just what the conditions are, as in climbing a steep and rough mountain where no trail has been laid out. Exercise of observation is, then, one condition of transformation of impulse into a purpose. As in the sign by a railway crossing, we have to stop, look, listen.

But observation alone is not enough. We have to understand the *significance* of what we see, hear, and touch. This significance consists

Chapter 6 The Meaning of Purpose

of the consequences that will result when what is seen is acted upon. A baby may *see* the brightness of a flame and be attracted thereby to reach for it. The significance of the flame is then not its brightness but its power to burn, as the consequence that will result from touching it. We can be aware of consequences only because of previous experiences. In cases that are familiar because of many prior experiences we do not have to stop to remember just what those experiences were. A flame comes to signify light and heat without our having expressly to think of previous experiences of heat and burning. But in unfamiliar cases, we cannot tell just what the consequences of observed conditions will be unless we go over past experiences in our mind, unless we reflect upon them and by seeing what is similar in them to those now present, go on to form a judgment of what may be expected in the present situation.

The formation of purposes is, then, a rather complex intellectual operation. It involves (1) observation of surrounding conditions; (2) knowledge of what has happened in similar situations in the past, a knowledge obtained partly by recollection and partly from the information, advice, and warning of those who have had a wider experience; and (3) judgment which puts together what is observed and what is recalled to see what they signify. A purpose differs from an original impulse and desire through its translation into a plan and method of action based upon foresight of the consequences of acting under given observed conditions in a certain way. "If wishes were horses, beggars would ride." Desire for something may be intense. It may be so strong as to override estimation of the consequences that will follow acting upon it. Such occurrences do not provide the model for education. The crucial educational problem is that of procuring the postponement of immediate action upon desire until observation and judgment have intervened. Unless I am mistaken, this point is definitely relevant to the conduct of progressive schools. Overemphasis upon activity as an end, instead of upon *intelligent* activity, leads to identification of freedom with immediate execution of impulses and desires. This identification is justified by a confusion of impulse with purpose; although, as has just been said, there is no purpose unless overt action is postponed until there is foresight of the consequences of carrying the impulse into execution — a foresight that is impossible without observation, information, and judgment. Mere foresight, even if it takes the form of accurate prediction, is not, of course, enough. The intellectual anticipation, the idea of consequences, must blend with desire and impulse to acquire moving force. It then gives direction to what otherwise is blind, while desire gives ideas impetus and momentum. An idea then becomes a plan in and for an activity to be carried out. Suppose a man has a desire to secure a new home, say by building a house. No matter how strong his desire, it cannot be directly executed. The man must form an idea of what kind of house he wants, including the number and arrangement of rooms, etc. He has to draw a plan, and have blue prints and specifications made. All this might be an idle amusement for spare time unless he also took stock of his resources. He must consider the relation of his funds and available credit to the execution of the plan. He has to investigate available sites, their price, their nearness to his place of business, to a congenial neighborhood, to school facilities, and so on and so on. All of the things reckoned with: his ability to pay, size and needs of family, possible locations, etc., etc., are objective facts. They are no part of the original desire. But they have to be viewed and judged in order that a desire may be converted into a purpose and a purpose into a plan of action.

All of us have desires, all at least who have not become so pathological that they are completely apathetic. These desires are the ultimate moving springs of action. A professional businessman wishes to succeed in his career; a general wishes to win the battle; a parent to have a comfortable home for his family, and to educate his children, and so on indefinitely. The intensity of the desire measures the strength of the efforts that will be put forth. But the wishes are empty castles in the air unless they are translated into the means by which they may be realized. The question of *how soon* or of means takes the place of a projected imaginative end, and, since means are objective, they have to be studied and understood if a genuine purpose is to be formed.

Traditional education tended to ignore the importance of personal impulse and desire as moving springs. But this is no reason why progressive education should identify impulse and desire with purpose and thereby pass lightly over the need for careful observation, for wide range of information, and for judgment if students are to share in the formation of the purposes which activate them. In an *educational* scheme, the occurrence of a desire and impulse is not the final end. It is an occasion and a demand for the formation of a plan and method of activity. Such a plan, to repeat, can be formed only by study of conditions and by securing all relevant information.

The teacher's business is to see that the occasion is taken advantage of. Since freedom resides in the operations of intelligent observation and judgment by which a purpose is developed, guidance given by the teacher to the exercise of the pupils' intelligence is an aid to freedom, not a restriction upon it. Sometimes teachers seem to be afraid even to make suggestions to the members of a group as to what they should do. I have heard of cases in which children are surrounded with objects and materials and then left entirely to themselves, the teacher being loath to suggest even what might be done with the materials lest freedom be infringed upon. Why, then, even supply materials, since they are a source of some suggestion or other? But what is more important is that the suggestion upon which pupils act must in any case come from somewhere. It is impossible to

Chapter 6 The Meaning of Purpose

understand why a suggestion from one who has a larger experience and a wider horizon should not be at least as valid as a suggestion arising from some more or less accidental source.

It is possible of course to abuse the office, and to force the activity of the young into channels which express the teacher's purpose rather than that of the pupils. But the way to avoid this danger is not for the adult to withdraw entirely. The way is, first, for the teacher to be intelligently aware of the capacities, needs, and past experiences of those under instruction, and, secondly, to allow the suggestion made to develop into a plan and project by means of the further suggestions contributed and organized into a whole by the members of the group. The plan, in other words, is a co-operative enterprise, not a dictation. The teacher's suggestion is not a mold for a cast-iron result but is a starting point to be developed into a plan through contributions from the experience of all engaged in the learning process. The development occurs through reciprocal give-and-take, the teacher taking but not being afraid also to give. The essential point is that the purpose grow and take shape through the process of social intelligence.

CHAPTER 7

PROGRESSIVE ORGANIZATION OF SUBJECT-MATTER

Allusion has been made in passing a number of times to objective conditions involved in experience and to their function in promoting or failing to promote the enriched growth of further experience. By implication, these objective conditions, whether those of observation, of memory, of information procured from others, or of imagination, have been identified with the subject-matter of study and learning; or, speaking more generally, with the stuff of the course of study. Nothing, however, has been said explicitly so far about subject-matter as such. That topic will now be discussed. One consideration stands dearly when education is conceived in terms of experience. Anything which can be called a study, whether arithmetic, history, geography, or one of the natural sciences, must be derived from materials which at the outset fall within the scope of ordinary life-experience. In this respect the newer education contrasts sharply with procedures which start with facts and truths that are outside the range of the experience of those taught, and which, therefore, have the problem of discovering ways and means of bringing them within experience. Undoubtedly one chief cause for the great success of newer methods in early elementary education has been its observance of the contrary principle.

But finding the material for learning within experience is only the first step. The next step is the progressive development of what is already experienced into a fuller and richer and also more organized form, a form that gradually approximates that in which subject-matter is presented to the skilled, mature person. That this change is possible without departing from the organic connection of education with experience is shown by the fact that this change takes place outside of the school and apart from formal education. The infant, for example, begins with an environment of objects that is very restricted in space and time. That environment steadily expands by the momentum inherent in experience itself without aid from scholastic instruction. As the infant learns to reach, creep, walk, and talk, the intrinsic subject-matter of its experience widens and deepens. It comes into connection with new objects and events which call out new powers, while the exercise of these powers refines and enlarges the content of its experience. Life-space and life-durations are expanded. The environment, the world of experience, constantly grows larger and,

Chapter 7 Progressive Organization of Subject-Matter

so to speak, thicker. The educator who receives the child at the end of this period has to find ways for doing consciously and deliberately what "nature" accomplishes in the earlier years.

It is hardly necessary to insist upon the first of the two conditions which have been specified. It is a cardinal precept of the newer school of education that the beginning of instruction shall be made with the experience learners already have; that this experience and the capacities that have been developed during its course provide the starting point for all further learning. I am not so sure that the other condition, that of orderly development toward expansion and organization of subject-matter through growth of experience, receives as much attention. Yet the principle of continuity of educative experience requires that equal thought and attention be given to solution of this aspect of the educational problem. Undoubtedly this phase of the problem is more difficult than the other. Those who deal with the pre-school child, with the kindergarten child, and with the boy and girl of the early primary years do not have much difficulty in determining the range of past experience or in finding activities that connect in vital ways with it. With older children both factors of the problem offer increased difficulties to the educator. It is harder to find out the background of the experience of individuals and harder to find out just how the subject-matters already contained in that experience shall be directed so as to lead out to larger and better organized fields.

It is a mistake to suppose that the principle of the leading on of experience to something different is adequately satisfied simply by giving pupils some new experiences any more than it is by seeing to it that they have greater skill and ease in dealing with things with which they are already familiar. It is also essential that the new objects and events be related intellectually to those of earlier experiences, and this means that there be some advance made in conscious articulation of facts and ideas. It thus becomes the office of the educator to select those things within the range of existing experience that have the promise and potentiality of presenting new problems which by stimulating new ways of observation and judgment will expand the area of further experience. He must constantly regard what is already won not as a fixed possession but as an agency and instrumentality for opening new fields which make new demands upon existing powers of observation and of intelligent use of memory. Connectedness in growth must be his constant watchword.

The educator more than the member of any other profession is concerned to have a long look ahead. The physician may feel his job done when he has restored a patient to health. He has undoubtedly the obligation of advising him how to live so as to avoid similar troubles in the future. But, after all, the conduct of his life is his own affair, not the physician's; and what is more important for the present point is that as far as the physician does occupy himself

Chapter 7 Progressive Organization of Subject-Matter

with instruction and advice as to the future of his patient he takes upon himself the function of an educator. The lawyer is occupied with winning a suit for his client or getting the latter out of some complication into which he has got himself. If it goes beyond the case presented to him he too becomes an educator. The educator by the very nature of his work is obliged to see his present work in terms of what it accomplishes, or fails to accomplish, for a future whose objects are linked with those of the present.

Here, again, the problem for the progressive educator is more difficult than for the teacher in the traditional school. The latter had indeed to look ahead. But unless his personality and enthusiasm took him beyond the limits that hedged in the traditional school, he could content himself with thinking of the next examination period or the promotion to the next class. He could envisage the future in terms of factors that lay within the requirements of the school system as that conventionally existed. There is incumbent upon the teacher who links education and actual experience together a more serious and a harder business. He must be aware of the potentialities for leading students into new fields which belong to experiences already had, and must use this knowledge as his criterion for selection and arrangement of the conditions that influence their present experience.

Because the studies of the traditional school consisted of subject-matter that was selected and arranged on the basis of the judgment of adults as to what would be useful for the young sometime in the future, the material to be learned was settled upon outside the present life-experience of the learner. In consequence, it had to do with the past; it was such as had proved useful to men in past ages. By reaction to an opposite extreme, as unfortunate as it was probably natural under the circumstances, the sound idea that education should derive its materials from present experience and should enable the learner to cope with the problems of the present and future has often been converted into the idea that progressive schools can to a very large extent ignore the past. If the present could be cut off from the past, this conclusion would be sound. But the achievements of the past provide the only means at command for understanding the present. Just as the individual has to draw in memory upon his own past to understand the conditions in which he individually finds himself, so the issues and problems of present *social* life are in such intimate and direct connection with the past that students cannot be prepared to understand either these problems or the best way of dealing with them without delving into their roots in the past. In other words, the sound principle that the objectives of learning are in the future and its immediate materials are in present experience can be carried into effect only in the degree that present experience is stretched, as it were, backward. It can expand into the future only as it is also enlarged to take in the past.

Chapter 7 Progressive Organization of Subject-Matter

If time permitted, discussion of the political and economic issues which the present generation will be compelled to face in the future would render this general statement definite and concrete. The nature of the issues cannot be understood save as we know how they came about. The institutions and customs that exist in the present and that give rise to present social ills and dislocations did not arise overnight. They have a long history behind them. Attempt to deal with them simply on the basis of what is obvious in the present is bound to result in adoption of superficial measures which in the end will only render existing problems more acute and more difficult to solve. Policies framed simply upon the ground of knowledge of the present cut off from the past is the counterpart of heedless carelessness in individual conduct. The way out of scholastic systems that made the past an end in itself is to make acquaintance with the past a *means* of understanding the present. Until this problem is worked out, the present clash of educational ideas and practices will continue. On the one hand, there will be reactionaries that claim that the main, if not the sole, business of education is transmission of the cultural heritage. On the other hand, there will be those who hold that we should ignore the past and deal only with the present and future.

That up to the present time the weakest point in progressive schools is in the matter of selection and organization of intellectual subject-matter is, I think, inevitable under the circumstances. It is as inevitable as it is right and proper that they should break loose from the cut and dried material which formed the staple of the old education. In addition, the field of experience is very wide and it varies in its contents from place to place and from time to time. A single course of studies for all progressive schools is out of the question; it would mean abandoning the fundamental principle of connection with life-experiences. Moreover, progressive schools are new. They have had hardly more than a generation in which to develop. A certain amount of uncertainty and of laxity in choice and organization of subject-matter is, therefore, what was to be expected. It is no ground for fundamental criticism or complaint.

It is a ground for legitimate criticism, however, when the ongoing movement of progressive education fails to recognize that the problem of selection and organization of subject-matter for study and learning is fundamental. Improvisation that takes advantage of special occasions prevents teaching and learning from being stereotyped and dead. But the basic material of study cannot be picked up in a cursory manner. Occasions which are not and cannot be foreseen are bound to arise wherever there is intellectual freedom. They should be utilized. But there is a decided difference between using them in the development of a continuing line of activity and trusting to them to provide the chief material of learning.

Chapter 7 Progressive Organization of Subject-Matter

Unless a given experience leads out into a field previously unfamiliar no problems arise, while problems are the stimulus to thinking. That the conditions found in present experience should be used as sources of problems is a characteristic which differentiates education based upon experience from traditional education. For in the latter, problems were set from outside. Nonetheless, growth depends upon the presence of difficulty to be overcome by the exercise of intelligence. Once more, it is part of the educator's responsibility to see equally to two things: First, that the problem grows out of the conditions of the experience being had in the present, and that it is within the range of the capacity of students; and, secondly, that it is such that it arouses in the learner an active quest for information and for production of new ideas. The new facts and new ideas thus obtained become the ground for further experiences in which new problems are presented. The process is a continuous spiral. The inescapable linkage of the present with the past is a principle whose application is not restricted to a study of history. Take natural science, for example. Contemporary social life is what it is in very large measure because of the results of application of physical science. The experience of every child and youth, in the country and the city, is what it is in its present actuality because of appliances which utilize electricity, heat, and chemical processes. A child does not eat a meal that does not involve in its preparation and assimilation chemical and physiological principles. He does not read by artificial light or take a ride in a motor car or on a train without coming into contact with operations and processes which science has engendered.

It is a sound educational principle that students should be introduced to scientific subject-matter and be initiated into its facts and laws through acquaintance with everyday social applications. Adherence to this method is not only the most direct avenue to understanding of science itself but as the pupils grow more mature it is also the surest road to the understanding of the economic and industrial problems of present society. For they are the products to a very large extent of the application of science in production and distribution of commodities and services, while the latter processes are the most important factor in determining the present relations of human beings and social groups to one another. It is absurd, then, to argue that processes similar to those studied in laboratories and institutes of research are not a part of the daily life experience of the young and hence do not come within the scope of education based upon experience. That the immature cannot study scientific facts and principles in the way in which mature experts study them goes without saying. But this fact, instead of exempting the educator from responsibility for using present experiences so that learners may gradually be led, through extraction of facts and laws, to experience of a scientific order, sets one of his main problems.

Chapter 7 Progressive Organization of Subject-Matter

For if it is true that existing experience in detail and also on a wide scale is what it is because of the application of science, first, to processes of production and distribution of goods and services, and then to the relations which human beings sustain socially to one another, it is impossible to obtain an understanding of present social forces (without which they cannot be mastered and directed) apart from an education which leads learners into knowledge of the very same facts and principles which in their final organization constitute the sciences. Nor does the importance of the principle that learners should be led to acquaintance with scientific subject-matter cease with the insight thereby given into present social issues. The methods of science also point the way to the measures and policies by means of which a better social order can be brought into existence. The applications of science which have produced in large measure the social conditions which now exist do not exhaust the possible field of their application. For so far science has been applied more or less casually and under the influence of ends, such as private advantage and power, which are a heritage from the institutions of a prescientific age.

We are told almost daily and from many sources that it is impossible for human beings to direct their common life intelligently. We are told, on one hand, that the complexity of human relations, domestic and international, and on the other hand, the fact that human beings are so largely creatures of emotion and habit, make impossible large-scale social planning and direction by intelligence. This view would be more credible if any systematic effort, beginning with early education and carried on through the continuous study and learning of the young, had ever been undertaken with a view to making the method of intelligence, exemplified in science, supreme in education. There is nothing in the inherent nature of habit that prevents intelligent method from becoming itself habitual; and there is nothing in the nature of emotion to prevent the development of intense emotional allegiance to the method.

The case of science is here employed as an illustration of progressive selection of subject-matter resident in present experience towards organization: an organization which is free, not externally imposed, because it is in accord with the growth of experience itself. The utilization of subject-matter found in the present life-experience of the learner towards science is perhaps the best illustration that can be found of the basic principle of using existing experience as the means of carrying learners on to a wider, more refined, and better organized environing world, physical and human, than is found in the experiences from which educative growth sets out. Hogben's recent work, *Mathematics for the Million*, shows how mathematics, if it is treated as a mirror of civilization and as a main agency in its progress, can contribute to the desired goal as surely as can the physical

Chapter 7 Progressive Organization of Subject-Matter

sciences. The underlying ideal in any case is that of progressive organization of knowledge. It is with reference to organization of knowledge that we are likely to find *Either-Or* philosophies most acutely active. In practice, if not in so many words, it is often held that since traditional education rested upon a conception of organization of knowledge that was almost completely contemptuous of living present experience, therefore education based upon living experience should be contemptuous of the organization of facts and ideas.

When a moment ago I called this organization an *ideal*, I meant, on the negative side, that the educator cannot start with knowledge already organized and proceed to ladle it out in doses. But as an ideal the active process of organizing facts and ideas is an ever-present educational process. No experience is educative that does not tend both to knowledge of more facts and entertaining of more ideas and to a better, a more orderly, arrangement of them. It is not true that organization is a principle foreign to experience. Otherwise experience would be so dispersive as to be chaotic. The experience of young children centers about persons and the home. Disturbance of the normal order of relationships in the family is now known by psychiatrists to be a fertile source of later mental and emotional troubles — a fact which testifies to the reality of this kind of organization. One of the great advances in early school education, in the kindergarten and early grades, is that it preserves the social and human center of the organization of experience, instead of the older violent shift of the center of gravity. But one of the outstanding problems of education, as of music, is modulation. In the case of education, modulation means movement from a social and human center toward a more objective intellectual scheme of organization, always bearing in mind, however, that intellectual organization is not an end in itself but is the means by which social relations, distinctively human ties and bonds, may be understood and more intelligently ordered.

When education is based in theory and practice upon experience, it goes without saying that the organized subject-matter of the adult and the specialist cannot provide the starting point. Nevertheless, it represents the goal toward which education should continuously move. It is hardly necessary to say that one of the most fundamental principles of the scientific organization of knowledge is the principle of cause-and-effect. The way in which this principle is grasped and formulated by the scientific specialist is certainly very different from the way in which it can be approached in the experience of the young. But neither the relation nor grasp of its meaning is foreign to the experience of even the young child. When a child two or three years of age learns not to approach a flame too closely and yet to draw near enough a stove to get its warmth he is grasping and using the causal relation. There is no intelligent activity that does not conform to the

Chapter 7   Progressive Organization of Subject-Matter

requirements of the relation, and it is intelligent in the degree in which it is not only conformed to but consciously borne in mind.

In the earlier forms of experience the causal relation does not offer itself in the abstract but in the form of the relation of means employed to ends attained; of the relation of means and consequences. Growth in judgment and understanding is essentially growth in ability to form purposes and to select and arrange means for their realization. The most elementary experiences of the young are filled with cases of the means-consequence relation. There is not a meal cooked nor a source of illumination employed that does not exemplify this relation. The trouble with education is not the absence of situations in which the causal relation is exemplified in the relation of means and consequences. Failure to utilize the situations so as to lead the learner on to grasp the relation in the given cases of experience is, however, only too common. The logician gives the names "analysis and synthesis" to the operations by which means are selected and organized in relation to a purpose.

This principle determines the ultimate foundation for the utilization of *activities* in school. Nothing can be more absurd educationally than to make a plea for a variety of active occupations in the school while decrying the need for progressive organization of information and ideas. Intelligent activity is distinguished from aimless activity by the fact that it involves selection of means — analysis — out of the variety of conditions that are present, and their arrangement — synthesis — to reach an intended aim or purpose. That the more immature the learner is, the simpler must be the ends held in view and the more rudimentary the means employed, is obvious. But the principle of organization of activity in terms of some perception of the relation of consequences to means applies even with the very young. Otherwise an activity ceases to be educative because it is blind. With increased maturity, the problem of interrelation of means becomes more urgent. In the degree in which intelligent observation is transferred from the relation of means to ends to the more complex question of the relation of means to one another, the idea of cause and effect becomes prominent and explicit. The final justification of shops, kitchens, and so on in the school is not just that they afford opportunity for activity, but that they provide opportunity for the *kind* of activity or for the acquisition of mechanical skills which leads students to attend to the relation of means and ends, and then to consideration of the way things interact with one another to produce definite effects. It is the same in principle as the ground for laboratories in scientific research.

Unless the problem of intellectual organization can be worked out on the ground of experience, reaction is sure to occur toward externally imposed methods of organization. There are signs of this reaction already in evidence. We are told that our schools, old and

Chapter 7 Progressive Organization of Subject-Matter

new, are failing in the main task. They do not develop, it is said, the capacity for critical discrimination and the ability to reason. The ability to think is smothered, we are told, by accumulation of miscellaneous ill-digested information, and by the attempt to acquire forms of skill which will be immediately useful in the business and commercial world. We are told that these evils spring from the influence of science and from the magnification of present requirements at the expense of the tested cultural heritage from the past. It is argued that science and its method must be subordinated; that we must return to the logic of ultimate first principles expressed in the logic of Aristotle and St. Thomas, in order that the young may have sure anchorage in their intellectual and moral life, and not be at the mercy of every passing breeze that blows.

If the method of science had ever been consistently and continuously applied throughout the day-by-day work of the school in all subjects, I should be more impressed by this emotional appeal than I am. I see at bottom but two alternatives between which education must choose if it is not to drift aimlessly. One of them is expressed by the attempt to induce educators to return to the intellectual methods and ideals that arose centuries before scientific method was developed. The appeal may be temporarily successful in a period when general insecurity, emotional and intellectual as well as economic, is rife. For under these conditions the desire to lean on fixed authority is active. Nevertheless, it is so out of touch with all the conditions of modern life that I believe it is folly to seek salvation in this direction. The other alternative is systematic utilization of scientific method as the pattern and ideal of intelligent exploration and exploitation of the potentialities inherent in experience.

The problem involved comes home with peculiar force to progressive schools. Failure to give constant attention to development of the intellectual content of experiences and to obtain ever-increasing organization of facts and ideas may in the end merely strengthen the tendency toward a reactionary return to intellectual and moral authoritarianism. The present is not the time nor place for a disquisition upon scientific method. But certain features of it are so closely connected with any educational scheme based upon experience that they should be noted.

In the first place, the experimental method of science attaches more importance, not less, to ideas as ideas than do other methods. There is no such thing as experiment in the scientific sense unless action is directed by some leading idea. The fact that the ideas employed are hypotheses, not final truths, is the reason why ideas are more jealously guarded and tested in science than anywhere else. The moment they are taken to be first truths in themselves there ceases to be any reason for scrupulous examination of them. As fixed truths they must be accepted and that is the end of the matter. But as hypotheses, they must be continuously tested and revised, a requirement that demands they be accurately formulated.

In the second place, ideas or hypotheses are tested by the consequences which they produce when they are acted upon. This fact means that the consequences of action must be carefully and discriminatingly observed. Activity that is not checked by observation of what follows from it may be temporarily enjoyed. But intellectually it leads nowhere. It does not provide knowledge about the situations in which action occurs nor does it lead to clarification and expansion of ideas.

In the third place, the method of intelligence manifested in the experimental method demands keeping track of ideas, activities, and observed consequences. Keeping track is a matter of reflective review and summarizing, in which there is both discrimination and record of the significant features of a developing experience. To reflect is to look back over what has been done so as to extract the net meanings which are the capital stock for intelligent dealing with further experiences. It is the heart of intellectual organization and of the disciplined mind.

I have been forced to speak in general and often abstract

language. But what has been said is organically connected with the requirement that experiences in order to be educative must lead out into an expanding world of subject-matter, a subject-matter of facts or information and of ideas. This condition is satisfied only as the educator views teaching and learning as a continuous process of reconstruction of experience. This condition in turn can be satisfied only as the educator has a long look ahead, and views every present experience as a moving force in influencing what future experiences will be. I am aware that the emphasis I have placed upon scientific method may be misleading, for it may result only in calling up the special technique of laboratory research as that is conducted by specialists. But the meaning of the emphasis placed upon scientific method has little to do with specialized techniques. It means that scientific method is the only authentic means at our command for getting at the significance of our everyday experiences of the world in which we live. It means that scientific method provides a working pattern of the way in which and the conditions under which experiences are used to lead ever onward and outward. Adaptation of the method to individuals of various degrees of maturity is a problem for the educator, and the constant factors in the problem are the formation of ideas, acting upon ideas, observation of the conditions which result, and organization of facts and ideas for future use. Neither the ideas, nor the activities, nor the observations, nor the organization are the same for a person six years old as they are for one twelve or

Chapter 7　Progressive Organization of Subject-Matter

eighteen years old, to say nothing of the adult scientist. But at every level there is an expanding development of experience if experience is educative in effect. Consequently, whatever the level of experience, we have no choice but either to operate in accord with the pattern it provides or else to neglect the place of intelligence in the development and control of a living and moving experience.

CHAPTER 8

EXPERIENCE—THE MEANS AND GOAL OF EDUCATION

In what I have said I have taken for granted the soundness of the principle that education in order to accomplish its ends both for the individual learner and for society must be based upon experience — which is always the actual life-experience of some individual. I have not argued for the acceptance of this principle nor attempted to justify it. Conservatives as well as radicals in education are profoundly discontented with the present educational situation taken as a whole. There is at least this much agreement among intelligent persons of both schools of educational thought. The educational system must move one way or another, either backward to the intellectual and moral standards of a pre-scientific age or forward to ever greater utilization of scientific method in the development of the possibilities of growing, expanding experience. I have but endeavored to point out some of the conditions which must be satisfactorily fulfilled if education takes the latter course.

For I am so confident of the potentialities of education when it is treated as intelligently directed development of the possibilities inherent in ordinary experience that I do not feel it necessary to criticize here the other route nor to advance arguments in favor of taking the route of experience. The only ground for anticipating failure in taking this path resides to my mind in the danger that experience and the experimental method will not be adequately conceived. There is no discipline in the world so severe as the discipline of experience subjected to the tests of intelligent development and direction. Hence the only ground I can see for even a temporary reaction against the standards, aims, and methods of the newer education is the failure of educators who professedly adopt them to be faithful to them in practice. As I have emphasized more than once, the road of the new education is not an easier one to follow than the old road but a more strenuous and difficult one. It will remain so until it has attained its majority and that attainment will require many years of serious co-operative work on the part of its adherents. The greatest danger that attends its future is, I believe, the idea that it is an easy way to follow, so easy that its course may be improvised, if not in an impromptu fashion, at least almost from day to day or from week to week. It is for this reason that instead of extolling its principles, I have confined

Chapter 8　Experience—The Means and Goal of Education

myself to showing certain conditions which must be fulfilled if it is to have the successful career which by right belongs to it.

I have used frequently in what precedes the words "progressive" and "new" education. I do not wish to close, however, without recording my firm belief that the fundamental issue is not of new versus old education nor of progressive against traditional education but a question of what anything whatever must be to be worthy of the name *education*. I am not, I hope and believe, in favor of any ends or any methods simply because the name progressive may be applied to them. The basic question concerns the nature of education with no qualifying adjectives prefixed. What we want and need is education pure and simple, and we shall make surer and faster progress when we devote ourselves to finding out just what education is and what conditions have to be satisfied in order that education may be a reality and not a name or a slogan. It is for this reason alone that I have emphasized the need for a sound philosophy of experience.

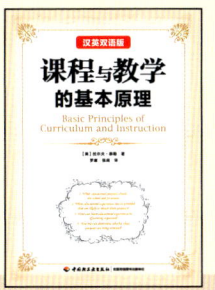

¥42.00

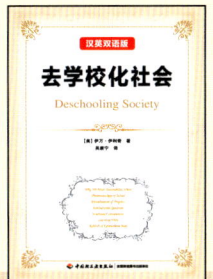

¥58.00

《课程与教学的基本原理》（汉英双语版）
【美】拉尔夫·泰勒 著
罗康 等 译

"现代课程理论之父"泰勒的代表作，被誉为"现代课程理论的'圣经'"。高等院校教育专业师生和中小学教师的必读经典。

《去学校化社会》（汉英双语版）
【美】伊万·伊利奇 著
吴康宁 译

当代著名教育思想家伊万·伊利奇的代表作。著名教育社会学者吴康宁教授倾情翻译并解读这一思想巨著。

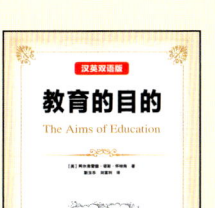

¥48.00

¥58.00

《教育的目的》（汉英双语版）
【英】阿尔弗雷德·诺斯·怀特海 著
靳玉乐 等 译

英国哲学家、教育家和数学家怀特海的教育代表作。著名教育学者靳玉乐教授等翻译，译者注释丰富，汉英双语对照，十分有助于品味经典。

《论教育学·系科之争》
【德】伊曼努埃尔·康德 著
杨云飞 邓晓芒 译／邓晓芒 校

全面地反映了德国哲学家和教育家康德的教育思想。我国著名哲学家邓晓芒教授和其弟子杨云飞博士根据德文原著历时一年多精心翻译。

¥48.00

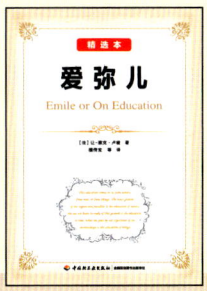

¥48.00

《大教学论》（评注版）
【捷】约翰·阿莫斯·夸美纽斯 著
刘富利 等 译

捷克教育家夸美纽斯的代表作，标志着教学论的诞生。牛津大学教育学者莫里斯·沃尔特·基廷在书中做出了精彩的评论。

《爱弥儿》（精选本）
【法】让-雅克·卢梭 著
檀传宝 等 译

法国启蒙思想家和教育家卢梭的代表作，一本小说体教育名著。著名教育学者檀传宝教授领衔选译《爱弥儿》全书的精华部分。

"世界教育经典名著丛书"阅读推广计划

尊敬的老师:

您好!感谢您对"万千教育"的关注与支持!

近年来,我们策划出版了"世界教育经典名著丛书"。该丛书包括16部世界著名的教育家、哲学家和心理学家的教育代表作,由国内十余位权威专家精心译校。大量的译者注和精彩的"译者导读"有助于读者领略名著的思想精髓。用纸考究、印刷清晰和软精装使丛书可读宜藏。我们有幸取得了数部著作在中国大陆的独家中文版权和英文版权。

其中《课程与教学的基本原理》《民主主义与教育》《教育的目的》《去学校化社会》《经验与教育》等7种名著采用了汉英双语的出版形式,可满足读者阅读原汁原味的经典之需。这些图书也适合作为高校师生专业外语教学文本。

为了让更多的人走近经典,值此"万千教育"编辑部成立20周年之际,我们制订了"世界教育经典名著丛书"阅读推广计划。

如果您对我们出版的经典名著感兴趣,我们将特别为您提供下列服务:

1. 免费样书。如果您选用上述名著作为教学文本或为了便于您推荐给学生阅读,我们可以免费向您提供教师样书。

2. 优惠折扣。若您所在院校的学生欲团购上述名著,我们将给予特定的优惠折扣。

欲了解"世界教育经典名著丛书"及阅读推广计划的详情,请扫描右边的二维码。此计划长期有效。

欢迎您与我们联系!

万千教育编辑部

咨询电话:010-65181109
读者邮箱:1012305542@qq.com
万千教育客服微信号:wqjy1998